becoming a friendly helper:

A Handbook
for Student Facilitators

by
Robert D. Myrick
and
Robert P. Bowman

Copyright © 1981
EDUCATIONAL MEDIA CORPORATION ®
P.O. Box 21311
Minneapolis, Minnesota 55421

Library of Congress Catalog Card No. 81-82899

ISBN 0-932796-08-7

Printing (Last Digit)

9 8 7 6 5 4 3

Production editor —

Don L. Sorenson

Graphic design—

Earl Sorenson

Illustrations—

Mary M. McKee

A Leadership Training Program for Young Students

(Grades 4 - 8)

Becoming a Friendly Helper (A book for students)
Children Helping Children (A book for trainers)

Becoming a Friendly Helper is a handbook designed for students grades four through eight participating in a peer facilitator training program. The companion book, *Children Helping Children*, is a trainer manual providing ideas for organizing a peer program, preparing student leaders, and supervising helping projects.

Dedicated to

Linda and Denise

two very special "friendly helpers"

Table of Contents

Introduction   **vii**

Chapter I:
  Friendly Helpers and Helping Characteristics   **1**
What You Will Learn From This Book   4
How To Use This Book   7
The Need For Friendly Help   9
    Activity 1.1: Who Needs Help?   13
    Activity 1.2: Who Are the Helpers?   14
Students as Friendly Helpers   15
The Helping Characteristics   17
Summary   19
    Activity 1.3: Feeling Word Search   20

Chapter II: The Careful Listener   **21**
Look At the Person Who is Talking   23
    Activity 2.1: Feeling Faces — Part I   24
Pay Attention to the Person's Words   26
    Activity 2.2: Key Words and Feelings   27
Be Aware of the Person's Feelings   29
Table 1: Pleasant and Unpleasant Feeling Words   30
    Activity 2.3: Feeling Faces — II   31
    Activity 2.4: Identifying Feelings   32
Say Something That Shows You Are Listening   33
Summary   34

Chapter III: Making Helpful Responses   **35**
Three Helpful Responses   45
Ask Open Questions   46
    Activity 3.1: Questioning a Friend   49
Clarify and Summarize the Ideas   50
    Activity 3.2: Clarifying and Summarizing Ideas   52
Focus on the Person's Feelings   53
    Activity 3.3: Feeling-Focused Responses   57
    Activity 3.4: Following Charlie's Talk   58
Summary   60

Chapter IV: Helping Solve Problems   **61**
Problems, Problems, Problems!   63
    Activity 4.1: Students Have Problems Too   64
A Problem-Solving Model   68
The Model: Five Important Questions   69
Summary   76

Chapter V: Giving Feedback   **79**
A Feedback Model   80
Using the Feedback Model   85
Family Feedback   86
    Activity 5.1: Some Feedback to Others   87
Feedback to Rod   88
Complimenting and Confronting Others   89
Summary   90
    Activity 5.2: Time for Another Compliment 90

Chapter VI: Looking at Yourself and Others   **91**
Your Self-Image   95
Your Physical Self   99
Your Beliefs and Attitudes   102
Your Skills and Abilities   103
Your Self With Others   105
Summary   107
    Activity 6.1: Looking at Your Self-Image 108
    Activity 6.2: Incomplete Sentences   110

Chapter VII: Becoming a Friendly Helper   **111**
Questions Facilitators Have Asked   115
You Can Make a Difference   117
Student Facilitator Merit Award   119

Introduction

This book is about helping. It will teach you how to receive and to give help. As you study it, you will learn some things about helping. You can become a better friend to others than you have ever been before.

You may be in a friendly helper program and studying this book in a training group. If so, you will practice some helping skills and then work in some helping projects. You can also use this book by yourself and try the ideas on your own. There will be many times when you can use what you learn, both at school and at home.

Like so many others your age, you can learn more about your feelings and ideas. You can also learn to solve problems, make responsible decisions, and help others to do the same. In schools across our great country, young people are learning more about themselves and others every day. They are learning to communicate. They are finding how nice it can be to have friendly helpers in life. All of us depend upon the good will and friendship of others. It makes life better when we know that friendly help is available.

After you read this book and take part in a training program, you can be a *facilitator* or friendly helper. You might work as an assistant to teachers and counselors, a tutor, a special friend, or a small group leader. You will learn more about these roles later.

The road to becoming a facilitator takes time and can be difficult. It is also interesting and fun. You are going to have rewarding moments that will make the journey worthwhile. Good luck on your way to becoming a friendly helper!

RDM
RPB

Chapter I

Friendly Helpers
and
Helping Characteristics

Sam was a small first grade student. One day he heard some boys yell at him, "Sammy is a carrot head—Sammy is a carrot head." Then the boys ran off to one side of the playground. Sam turned and ran in the other direction. He was afraid and wasn't sure what to do. After all, it wasn't his idea to have red hair. His father had red hair, but no one teased him. Sam secretly wished he were big and strong so he could "beat up" those boys. He'd teach them not to call him names.

But, today Sam felt small and weak. Sadness and worry showed on his face. He tried to hide from the boys behind the water fountain. What was he to do? He had already complained to the teacher, and she told the boys to leave him alone. But that didn't seem to matter. "Look out for the rabbits, Carrot Head," shouted one of the boys, as the others laughed. The water fountain wasn't big enough to protect him.

Nearby, Angie and her sixth grade friends were talking about their plans for Saturday afternoon. They could hear the boys teasing Sam. One girl told the boys to "go play somewhere else" because they were bothering her. Angie, however, could see that Sam was very sad. He looked lonely and hurt.

Becoming a Friendly Helper

Angie walked over to Sam and said, "Hi, you sure look sad right now. Things just don't seem to be going well for you." Sam looked at her and hung his head. "Nobody likes me," he finally said.

Angie left her friends and talked with Sam. She asked him about school, about what he liked to do, and about his plans for Saturday. As she talked with him, Sam became a little more relaxed. He forgot about the other boys for awhile. He liked talking with Angie. She was so friendly.

Then, the bell rang and both Sam and Angie said good-bye. They started back to their classrooms. As Sam walked through the doorway, he turned around one more time. He gave a little wave and smile to Angie, who turned out to be a needed friend at just the right time.

Angie was pleased with herself, too. She felt like a friendly helper. She also was proud to be able to use some of the ideas that she had learned as a student facilitator.

What is a student facilitator? A *student facilitator* is a student like you who uses special skills to help others think about their ideas and feelings. When you use these skills, you can help others to talk about themselves. You can also help them to solve their own problems. These skills can be learned by almost everyone. They can help you become a better friend to other students, teachers and parents. This book will help you to become a friendly helper, a student facilitator, like Angie.

What You Will Learn From This Book

Some of the things that you will learn from reading this book and from doing the activities are:

1. What kinds of problems other people have
2. What it takes to be a helper
3. How to be a better listener
4. What to say and do to make you a better helper
5. How to help others solve their own problems
6. How to use all of these ideas and more to become a friendly helper.

There are many students like you who have become facilitators and who have used the ideas in this book. Some have reported the successes they had with others. Some have told of the nice things that others have said about their help. However, almost all student facilitators agree that what they do is fun and that they also are helped in some special ways. Here are some things that student facilitators have said:

— "It makes me a better helper. I thought I was good at helping kids, but I'm a lot better now."

— "Other kids, and my teacher, respect me more. They think I am a good helper."

— "I like being a leader. Other students ask me for help now."

— "I learned that I'm not the only one who has problems."

— "I'm less afraid of people now. I also think I can solve problems of my own as they come up."

— "My grades improved. I think it's because I listen better than before."

— "My teacher told my parents that I am doing better in school since I was in the program. That's the first time she has said that about me."

— "I like it when I get to work with others. It makes me feel warm and happy inside. I like it best when I know I'm helping someone who needs it."

— "I got to be better friends with Tommy (another student facilitator)."

— "It was hard work some time, but most of the time it was fun."

— "I think if I had a problem and didn't know what to do, I would like to talk with a person who has learned what we have in this program."

— "The little kids were so cute. I was surprised how much they liked me.

Becoming a Friendly Helper

How To Use This Book

Working through this book can be like planting a fruit tree. The more effort and attention that you give to it at first, the more fruit it will give to you later. The ideas in this book are like tiny seeds. They need to be cared for before they will grow and bear fruit.

Study the ideas. Make them a part of yourself. Look carefully at the examples. Think of times when you might have noticed the same thing. When you come to questions and activities, take some time to think about them. They, too, can be little seeds that will grow some budding ideas and skills. Later, these ideas and skills will blossom. They can turn into fruitful moments with others that will be rewarding to you and to them.

After you have finished the studies in this book, you may call yourself a "student facilitator." Or, you may choose to use another name like "friendly helper" that tells others that you are now a skilled helper.

There is an award at the end of this book. When it is signed by you and your teacher or counselor, you will be one of some very special students who have learned the art of helping others.

LUNCHROOM ⇒

Becoming a Friendly Helper

The Need For Friendly Help

Everyone has problems. Almost every day things happen which cause problems for people. Many times help is needed before the problems can be solved.

Let's think of some times when someone can use help. A little boy who is feeling lost may look around. He wants help even though he's afraid to ask for it. When mothers and fathers are ill, help from the rest of the family is needed. A teacher who is worried about a student may want to talk with someone about the problem. Can you think of other times?

Some new students in your school might be unsure of themselves and seem shy. Some will need help in making new friends. Or, maybe they could use a friendly listener. Do you know of anyone your own age who is having problems in school? Perhaps that person could use some special help. Sometimes, we can't think of what to do when we have a problem. We might ask ourselves over and over, "What should we do?"

James, a fifth grade boy, was being teased about his clothes. His parents made him wear black shoes, striped socks, and black baggy pants. His stiff white shirts rubbed against his neck and made it sore. James wanted to obey his parents, but he wanted to wear clothes like the other boys in his class. He felt very sad and confused. James didn't know what to do.

Becoming a Friendly Helper

Sarah, a fifth grade girl, smiled often. Others thought she never had any problems. She was popular and did well with school work, but science was boring to her. She loved to play with Snowflake, her cat.

Snowflake had long soft white fur. She waited just inside the front door of the house for Sarah's return from school each day. One day, as Sarah walked through the door, she sensed that something was wrong. Her mother said that she had some sad news.

Snowflake had been hit by a car that morning and was dead. Sarah cried and cried. She grew very sad and lonely. The next day Sarah couldn't think about her school work, no matter how hard she tried. She needed someone who would listen to her. She needed a friend who could understand what she was feeling.

Both James and Sarah had problems. Each of them needed someone who would be a friend—someone who would show interest, understand, and care. They needed friendly help.

Let's look at some other examples. The following were said by other students. Friendly help was needed by each one.

- "I can't find my library book."

- "I don't get good enough grades for my parents."

- "I wish I were different."

- "The girl who sits behind me keeps getting me into trouble."

- "My parents are getting a divorce."

- "I'm afraid to walk home after school."

- "I'm lonely."

- "Things just don't ever seem to turn out right for me."

Who Needs Help ?

Activity 1.1

Think of a time when you noticed someone who needed help. What was the person thinking and feeling? In the space below, draw a picture that will help tell what happened.

Who Are the Helpers?

Activity 1.2

When we have a problem, there are several people who might help us. Read through the list and answer the questions that follow.

> Parent (or Guardian)
>
> Teacher
>
> Counselor
>
> Principal
>
> Nurse
>
> Police Officer
>
> Grandparent
>
> Neighbor
>
> Brother or Sister
>
> Friendly Student
>
> Stranger
>
> Other?

1. *Underline* each one you might go to for help, if you have a stomach ache.

2. *Put a star* in front of each one you might go to for help, if a group of kids started picking on you.

3. *Circle* each one you might go to for help, if you had some problems with math.

4. *Draw* a sad face after each one you might go to for help, if you were very lonely.

5. *Put an "X"* by each one you might go to for help, if someone in your class was telling lies about you.

Students as Friendly Helpers

How many times did you pick "friendly student?" Has another student ever asked you for help? Have you ever asked another student for help? Young people often seek out others near their own age when they want to talk about something that bothers them.

While adults can be very helpful, they are not always the first people students turn to for help. Some young people think adults are too busy and have little or no time for them. Some fear that their problems are not important enough to bother their parents or teachers. Others worry that adults may not understand. They are afraid to ask them for help. Still others like the friendship and help of someone their own age.

When we want help, we usually go to someone who makes us feel comfortable. Most of us feel better with friendly people. We don't want help from people who are bossy, pushy, or know-it-alls.

The best helpers have a lot of good ideas. But, above all, they also know how to help us talk about our problems. They want to know what is on our minds. *They take the time to hear us out, before they give their own ideas and suggestions.* They want to know about us.

Becoming a Friendly Helper

The Helping Characteristics

A lot is known about friendly helpers. The best helpers show some important characteristics when they are with others. Among these are four that you will want to think more about. If you want to be a friendly helper, then you will want to show that you are: (1) caring, (2) accepting, (3) understanding and (4) trustworthy. Let's look at each of these.

Caring. Friendly helpers show that they care about others by being interested in them. They are concerned about what is happening to other people.

You can show that you care about another person by being a "careful listener." Pay attention to the other person's ideas and feelings. Try not to interrupt. This could make the person think that you are not interested and that you don't care.

If you really care about the persons with whom you are talking, you will be open to their ideas. You will let them share a part of their lives. You will show that you care and they will feel closer to you than before.

Accepting. Friendly helpers respect other people. They accept people as worthwhile. You can show that you are accepting by trying to learn more about the other person's point of view. Try not to judge people as they share ideas with you. Avoid putting labels on them such as "bad," "goody-goody," "dumb," "stuck-up," "sissy," "brainy," and so on. Labels lump people together. They ignore personal worth.

An accepting helper values human beings. Yet, accepting someone does not mean that you must agree with what the person does or thinks. You may disagree with someone but still accept that person as worthy of your help.

Understanding. Friendly helpers are able to see things from the other person's point of view. They understand the person.

You can show your understanding by "tuning in" to a person's feelings, as well as ideas. You can listen to the story that the person is telling and find the most important thoughts and concerns. You may even be able to summarize them. You might also hear and tell the feelings that go with a story. This shows real understanding. The person you are helping will be impressed with your listening skill.

Trustworthy. Friendly helpers are seen by others as people who can be trusted. They say and do things that make others feel safe and secure.

You can show that you are trustworthy by keeping a person's ideas private. Others will learn that what they share with you will not be used against them. When they trust you with their thoughts, they might risk telling more about themselves. You could be a valuable key to help unlock problems and concerns when others know that you can keep a secret.

Do you think that Angie showed Sam these four characteristics when she talked with him? What do you think Angie did to help Sam talk about himself? Do you think Sam would like to talk with Angie again? Why?

Summary

To become a friendly helper, you will need to study about helpers and the skills they use. The more you study and practice, the more you will improve.

You are going to learn some new ideas and skills. Do you remember when you first learned to count? To learn the letters of the alphabet? It might have been difficult and even puzzling in the beginning. You may have wondered what it all meant. Yet, today, you use these basic skills to do math and to read books.

This book will give you some new skills for helping others. You can be a student facilitator—a friendly helper. Others your age have enjoyed being facilitators and have been helpful.

Will others want to talk with you? Can you learn to be more caring, accepting, understanding, and trustworthy? You are needed as a friendly helper. There are many people—both students and adults—who can use your help.

Friendly Helpers and Helping Characteristics

Feeling Word Search

Activity 1.3

Each letter below is part of one or more words which describe feelings. Words may be spelled forward, backward, up, down, or diagonally. Find each and circle it. See if you can

```
D  I  S  L  I  K  E  D
A  E  J  U  K  D  A  I
S  N  R  W  R  M  B  A
T  Z  G  O  Y  E  L  R
O  X  C  R  N  Q  E  F
H  A  P  P  Y  G  V  A
B  F  R  A  N  T  I  C
```

1. Disliked
2. Sad
3. Hot
4. Mad
5. Sure
6. Able
7. Happy
8. Frantic
9. Angry
10. Ignored
11. Afraid

Chapter II

The Careful Listener

Here are some things that have been said by teachers. Can you think of times when you might have heard similar things in your school?

— "Pay attention, now."

— "Everyone needs to listen now."

— "Who heard what David said?"

— "You're not listening very well."

— "Everyone is talking at the same time—take turns and the rest can listen."

— "If you'd only listen more then you wouldn't get in trouble."

— "Do I have to tell you the rules again? Okay, but listen carefully this time."

— "Quiet now, everybody listen."

Listening is one of the most important parts of learning. Those who learn to listen closely usually do well in school. They can follow directions better. They make fewer mistakes. Poor listeners, on the other hand, have more trouble understanding assignments and ideas. They often need to be told something more than once. A poor listener has more problems in school.

Poor listeners also have trouble making and keeping friends. For instance, Jeanne liked to talk about herself. She enjoyed telling others about the things she did and the thoughts she had. When others talked about their ideas, Jeanne would interrupt and start talking about herself again. Sometimes she acted as if she hadn't heard what others had said to her. She was thinking too much about herself. Jeanne was a poor listener.

Doing well in school and having close friends depends a lot on being a good listener. Yet, listening is something that most of us take little time to think about.

Students go to school to learn reading, writing, math, science, and other subjects. They seldom take time to learn listening skills. Yet, these skills can help all students have more success in school and with friends.

What is a good listener? Are you already a careful listener, or can you improve your listening habits? How can you know if you are really listening to someone? How can you tell if someone is listening clearly to you?

You will need to think more about the answers to these questions if you are going to be a friendly helper and a "facilitator." Let's begin by thinking more about listening habits and looking at four things that careful listeners do:

1. Look at the person who is talking.

2. Pay attention to the person's words.

3. Be aware of the person's feelings.

4. Say something that shows you are listening.

1. Look at the person who is talking. The careful listener looks at the person who is talking. It is possible to hear people without looking at them. But, listening and understanding are much easier when you look directly at the person who is talking. It is even better when you can see the person's face. The face can tell you a lot about what is being said. You can use your eyes, as well as your ears, to learn about people and their ideas. With practice you can almost "see" what people are thinking and feeling.

Teachers or friends might say to you, "Hey! Pay attention!" They probably want you to look at them or at whatever they are doing. They want your eyes on them. Your eyes will tell them whether you are interested or not. Your eyes tell them about your reactions. They give them clues as to what you are thinking.

Your eyes say a lot about you. When they are focused on people whom they are talking, they tell these persons that you are listening. You care enough to face them. You give them your attention. You want to hear what they have to say. This shows that they are important to you. Many people need good eye contact before they will warm up to you and see you as a friend and helper.

Feeling Faces — Part I

Activity 2.1

Look at the pictures of these boys and girls. What kinds of feelings do you think they are having? Under each picture are three feeling words that tell what the person might be feeling. Circle the one that you think *best* fits the picture. Put an "X" by the one that *least* fits the picture.

A.

_____ 1. Excited
_____ 2. Sad
_____ 3. Relaxed

B.

_____ 1. Shocked
_____ 2. Joyful
_____ 3. Bored

C.

_____ 1. Cheerful
_____ 2. Unsure
_____ 3. Angry

D.

_____ 1. Fascinated
_____ 2. Frustrated
_____ 3. Afraid

E.

_____ 1. Terrified
_____ 2. Nervous
_____ 3. Calm

F.

_____ 1. Confused
_____ 2. Angry
_____ 3. Grateful

2. Pay attention to the person's words. Careful listeners hold back their own ideas at first. They focus on what a talker is saying. Sometimes that's not easy.

As you listen to people talk you might think about many things. Their words can start you thinking about your own ideas. You can always share these later. To be a good listener you must keep your attention on the person talking.

Be patient with people who are talking to you. Give them time to tell what is on their minds. Let them be the center of attention.

It also might be helpful to listen for the main ideas that a person is talking about. Can you tell the ideas in your own words? Can you say them in such a way that the person would think, "Yes, that's what I was trying to say."? Listening for central ideas can be useful when a person has a lot to say. Try to remember a few key words and ideas.

Key Words and Feelings

Activity 2.2

There is more to listening than looking at a person and remembering what was said, that is a beginning. This activity can assist you to hear thoughts and feelings better.

Case No. 1 - Danny: "You know, the other day in art, Jim got me in trouble with the teacher. He said that I didn't clean up and that I was the one who left the brushes on the table. I was so mad at him. It was all I could do to keep from hitting him."

Which of the following *best* tells about the key idea Danny said? Underline it.

1. You made the teacher mad at you.
2. You left the paint brush out.
3. You didn't clean up.
4. You think that the teacher likes Jim best.
5. You don't like what Jim did.

Which of the following *best* tells what Danny might be *feeling* as he was telling his story. Underline it.

1. Excited
2. Happy
3. Angry
4. Scared
5. Lonely

Case No. 2 - Suzanne: "Have you studied for the test? What do you think Mrs. Adams (the teacher) might ask us? I studied a lot, but I'm still not sure about some of it. How do you think you'll do?"

Which of the following best tells what Suzanne said? Underline the key idea.

1. You are thinking a lot about the test.
2. You studied late last night.
3. You wish you could study some more.
4. You hate tests.
5. You don't like Mrs. Adams.

Which of the following best tells what Suzanne might be *feeling* as she was telling her story? Underline it.

1. Happy
2. Sad
3. Angry
4. Worried
5. Lonely

Becoming a Friendly Helper

3. Be aware of the person's feelings. Some people listen only to the exact words that are being said. They hear ideas, but they miss the feelings that go with the words. Feelings are a natural part of a person's life and they shouldn't be ignored.

Feelings are always part of us. Listen for them. Identify them. Remember how they fit with what the person is talking about.

Feelings are our emotions. If you are a careful listener, it is possible to hear a person's feelings—either pleasant or unpleasant. In fact, thinking about feelings in this way can help you to be a better listener. If you really want to show that you are a careful listener, then "tune in" to feelings.

Sometimes it will be worthwhile to think, "What am I hearing—pleasant or unpleasant feelings? Or, am I hearing both kinds of feelings?" Below is a list of *pleasant* and *unpleasant* feeling words. Why are some pleasant while others are unpleasant? How can you tell the difference?

Pleasant Feeling Words:	**Unpleasant Feeling Words:**
Happy	Sad
Glad	Angry
Thankful	Disappointed
Excited	Uncomfortable
Proud	

Some pleasant and unpleasant feeling words appear in Table 1. As you look at these words, which ones seem strange to you? Which ones are new to you? Which ones have you heard before? Can you think of some more feeling words to add to these lists?

Table 1

Pleasant and Unpleasant Feeling Words

Pleasant

Accepted	Enjoyment	Interested	Relaxed
Amused	Enthused	Involved	Relieved
Calm	Excited	Joyful	Safe
Certain	Fabulous	Liked	Satisfied
Challenged	Fascinated	Loved	Secure
Cheerful	Free	Neat	Settled
Comfortable	Friendly	Needed	Strong
Confident	Grateful	Peaceful	Super
Contented	Happy	Pleased	Sure
Cozy	Hopeful	Powerful	Touched
Delighted	Important	Proud	Trusted
Eager	Included	Refreshed	Unburdened
			Warm

Unpleasant

Afraid	Disappointed	Hopeless	Sad
Aggravated	Discouraged	Hurt	Scared
Alone	Disgusted	Left-out	Shocked
Angry	Distant	Lonely	Shy
Annoyed	Disturbed	Mad	Startled
Ashamed	Down	Miserable	Tearful
Bitter	Embarrassed	Mixed-up	Teased
Bored	Exhausted	Nervous	Tense
Cheated	Frightened	Put-down	Terrified
Confused	Frustrated	Rejected	Tired
Depressed	Furious	Restless	Worried
Desperate	Helpless		Worthless

Becoming a Friendly Helper

Feeling Faces — Part II

Activity 2.3

Look at the pictures below. How many of the faces show pleasant feelings and how many show unpleasant feelings? Beside each of the feeling words under the pictures, put a "P" for pleasant feelings and a "U" for unpleasant feelings.

A. _____   B. _____

C. _____   D. _____

E. _____   F. _____

The Lunchroom Line

Look at the picture of the lunchroom line. There are two groups of students. Each group is thinking about what they see. They are also showing some feelings. List three feeling words that you think might fit for each group.

Group 1 (the boys standing)

Feeling _____

Feeling _____

Feeling _____

Group 2 (the two girls)

Feeling _____

Feeling _____

Feeling _____

4. Say something that shows you are listening. You may look at someone and hear words and feelings. But, the person will not know if you are really listening unless you say something that shows it. Careful listeners are able to tell what they have heard. They know when it is their turn to talk. They don't change the subject. They stick to the point.

What a careful listener says also encourages the person to talk and think more about things. What they say shows the person that they understand and are interested.

Has there ever been a time in your life when a friend, teacher or parent didn't listen very well to you? How did it make you feel? Did you have pleasant or unpleasant feelings? Write those feeling words here:

_____

_____

_____

Think of a time when someone was a careful listener to you. How did that person pay attention to you? What kind of feelings did you have then? Write those feeling words here:

_____

_____

_____

Listening is not an easy job. To really listen you have to concentrate so that you can tell what you have heard. You will need the skills discussed here. You will also need to practice.

Summary

All people have thoughts and feelings. Listen for ideas but also be aware of pleasant and unpleasant feelings when someone is talking with you. This will help you tune-in and give you more understanding.

Listening is one of the most important parts of being a friendly helper. It can help you be more successful in school and with your friends. To be a careful listener, (1) look at the person who is talking; (2) pay attention to the person's words; (3) be aware of the person's feelings; and (4) say something that shows you are listening.

Becoming a Friendly Helper

Chapter III

Making Helpful Responses

"What should I say?" "What do I do now?" These questions are common to student facilitators who are learning how to help others. Listening is the first and most important part of helping people. But, a friendly listener must say something to "facilitate" them. What you say to someone may make a difference in whether you are helpful or not.

Here are some cases in which students are telling about problems. Read each case and write what you would say in that situation.

Case 1 - (Jeanne): Jeanne turns away from her friends and looks at the ground saying, "Well, I don't know. Maybe I could and maybe I coudn't...it's just that I've never tried to do something like that before."

What would you say? Write your response here:

_____

_____

_____

_____

_____

Becoming a Friendly Helper

Case 2 - (Paul): Paul is chasing after Roger. His fist is raised and he is shouting, "You dirty rat. . . if I ever catch you—you'll be sorry! You won't forget it either. . . ." Then, Paul slows down and walks over to you, still glaring and looking at Roger who has run away.

What would you say? Write your response here:

_____

_____

_____

_____

_____

In each of the two cases, what made you decide to say what you did? What were you hoping your words would do? How do you think Jeanne or Paul would feel about you?

There are many things that you could say in situations like Jeanne's and Paul's. What you say is your response to what is happening. Sometimes the words you speak can be helpful. At other times, your words may be less helpful. Sometimes they can even be hurtful. Let's take a closer look at what could be said in the two cases.

Look back at Case 1. Jeanne turned away from her friends and seemed afraid to try something new. She wasn't sure of herself. She might have been afraid of failing. Jeanne was having some unpleasant feelings at the time. Can you name some of them? Look at the unpleasant word list (Table 1 in Chapter II) and find some words that might tell what she was feeling. Write those words here:

_____

_____

_____

Some people might say to Jeanne, "Oh come on. It's not so hard and you can do it." This might encourage Jeanne. But, she is unsure of herself. She needs more than gentle support—she needs to feel accepted and understood.

Other people might say, "I did it and it was easy." In this case, the focus would be away from Jeanne and on someone else. It sends a message that Jeanne's feelings are unimportant. It says, "Don't feel the way you do. After all, I did it—be like me. It's easy!" Jeanne, of course, is thinking that what she faces doesn't seem easy. So, she may feel misunderstood or embarrassed because she is afraid.

Still other people, perhaps friendly helpers, would hear Jeanne's feelings and respond differently. They might say, "You're not sure you want to try." Then, they would pause and be silent for a moment. Keeping their eyes on Jeanne, they would wait for her to say something more. Jeanne might agree and talk a little more about her fears. Thus, this *feeling-focused response* would help Jeanne feel more understood and cared about.

Here are some more statements. Read the case of Jeanne again. Underline the statement that you would make.

Case 1 - (To Jeanne):

1. "You're unsure you want to try."

2. "It's not so hard and you can do it."

3. "What keeps you from trying it?"

4. "I did it and it was easy."

Let's look at these four responses again and imagine what would have happened if you had used them.

1. "You're unsure you want to try." In this response, you could see that she was feeling "unsure" of herself. "Unsure" is a *feeling word*. It shows her that you *understand.*

2. "It's not so hard and you can do it." This response shows you were trying to make her feel better. But, your support also ignores her feelings. This may be a better response later, after Jeanne thinks you understand her situation.

3. "What keeps you from trying it?" A question is asked. This may help her talk more. Yet, it doesn't show that you understand her feelings.

4. "I did it and it was easy." This response might even hurt. You put the focus on yourself and what you did. You also made her feelings of "not being sure" sound unimportant.

Case 2 - (To Paul): Read the case of Paul again and underline the statement that focuses on his feelings.

1. "You'd better be careful or you'll be in trouble, Paul."

2. "You're really mad, Paul."

3. "Hey, Paul, what happened between you and Roger?"

4. "I know just what you feel, Paul. Roger will be sorry someday."

Look now at these responses to Paul:

1. "You'd better be careful or you'll be in trouble, Paul." If you picked this response, you are giving him some advice. It might be helpful. But, he probably already knows what you've said. Your warning ignores his feelings.

2. "You're really mad, Paul." This response has a feeling word—"mad." You are showing that you heard some of his feelings. This is a *feeling-focused response.*

3. "Hey, Paul, what happened between you and Roger?" This is a question. It can help him talk some more. But, you are not showing that you understand his feelings at this point.

4. "I know just what you feel, Paul, and Roger will be sorry someday." Even though you say you know his feeling—there is no feeling word. That is not enough. In addition, the last part — "Roger will be sorry someday" — tells what *you* are thinking, not what Paul is feeling.

Here are two more cases. This time you will have some choices. You might not use the same words. Yet, if you were to speak, which responses would you choose?

Case 3 - (Diane): "My parents are going to be so mad when they get that note from Mrs. Jamison (her teacher). I'll have to stay at home for two weeks. I'll never get out to play. I'm really going to be in trouble when I get home."

Your response: Rank order the responses. Number the one you would choose first (1) and last (4).

_____(a) Talk with Mrs. Jamison and tell her how much trouble you will be in, if that note goes home.

_____(b) You're worried about what's going to happen when you get home.

_____(c) What do you think your parents will say to you?

_____(d) You are going to have to face up to your parents when you get home.

Case 4 - (Joe): "It's one of the best things that could happen to me. You see, I sold the most subscriptions for the paper this year. So, I get the free trip to Disney World."

Your Response: Rank order the responses. Mark those you would choose first (1) and last (4).

_____(a) Wow! Selling those subscriptions got you a real prize.

_____(b) Wow! How did you sell so many subscriptions?

_____(c) Wow! You sound so excited!

_____(d) Wow! I went to Disney World last year and it was fun.

There are many things that could be said to Diane and Joe. However, some very effective facilitators ranked their responses in this way:

For Diane:		For Joe:	
Rank	Response	Rank	Response
1.	B	1.	C
2.	D	2.	A
3.	C	3.	B
4.	A	4.	D

You may have an idea about why some responses were picked as "more facilitative" than others. When you read on and you will find some reasons that will explain the choices.

Three Helpful Responses

In Chapter I you learned about some important ideas about helpers. Friendly helpers are most helpful when they are seen by others as caring, accepting, understanding and trustworthy. What you say and do can determine whether or not others see you as friendly. One way to look at helping others is to ask: What must I do to be a helping person? What are some things I can say that will keep attention on the person I am working with?

There are three important kinds of helping responses that you can learn. You can use them to facilitate others to think about their ideas and feelings. These three responses are:

1. Ask open questions.

2. Clarify and summarize the ideas.

3. Focus on the person's feelings.

Ask Open Questions

There are many kinds of questions. Look at these:

1. Why did you do that?
2. What made you do that?
3. How did you do that?
4. When did you do that?
5. Where did you do that?
6. Who did you do that with?
7. Did you do that?
8. Are you going to do that again?

The first six questions ask the person to answer with more than a simple "yes" or "no." They are called *open questions* because they help "open up" the conversation. The person is encouraged to talk more. On the other hand, the last questions (7 and 8) are *closed questions.* They can be answered with a simple "yes" or "no." There is no need to explain more. The question has been answered and the conversation is closed.

Here are some examples of closed questions.

1. Do you like school?
2. Is that your book?
3. Did you study your lesson?
4. Did you do your homework?
5. Do you like him?
6. Are you going to the game?

If a person is unsure about talking with you, this kind of question is not very useful. Now, look at these open questions:

1. What do you like best (or least) about school?
2. What do you like to read?
3. How do you study your lesson?
4. What do you think about him?
5. How do you plan to do your homework?

The person must give more information. More words are needed to answer the questions.

Now, you try it. Write down a *closed question* and then an *open question* on the topic of school. Then do the same for the topic of friends. Look at the example about sports first.

Example: **Topic: Sports**

A Closed Question:

Do you like to watch sports?

An Open Question:

How do you feel about tennis?

Topic: School

Your Closed Question: _____

_____

Your Open Question: _____

_____

Topic: Friends

Your Closed Question: _____

_____

Your Open Question: _____

_____

One advantage is that a question keeps attention on the person you are trying to help. It asks that person to tell you more. It gives the person a chance to think more about ideas or problems. Your questions also show that you are interested. You are showing that you want to hear more. You are going to take some more time to listen.

Questioning a Friend

Activity 3.1

Sit in a circle with other students. Someone in the group volunteers to start. That person briefly tells something that has happened at school or at home.

Begin with the person on the left of the volunteer. Go around the circle while each member *asks the volunteer either a closed or an open question* about what was said. The volunteer does not answer the question, but *tells what kind of question was asked.*

Then, another volunteer takes a turn. Again, questions are asked of the volunteer, who names them as either open or closed questions.

Clarify and Summarize the Ideas

Questions can help a person talk more. But, nobody wants to spend a lot of time talking with someone who asks too many questions. Suppose that a person just asks questions and nothing else. That person may be seen as someone who is trying to be a detective —someone who just wants the facts of the case. Interest in the person is not shown.

Clarifying or *summarizing* what people say is one way of telling them that you are listening. It also helps them to hear what they have been saying to you. It is as if you took a picture with a camera. By clarifying or repeating ideas, you can give them a picture of what they said. They can think about or study the picture you show them and learn more about themselves.

Look at these statements:

Example 1: "Correct me if I am wrong. I heard you saying that getting good grades is more important to your parents than to you."

Example 2: "You seem to be saying that you would like to have more time to play."

Example 3: "Let me see if I am following you. You said that you were going to change schools next week."

When you clarify or summarize, try to repeat the main ideas. This helps focus the discussion by picking out some important things that are being said. Look at these summarizing statements:

Example 1: "Let's see now, you said that you want to get better grades and that you need to study more. You also said that you'd have to study more at home."

Example 2: "I'm hearing two important ideas from what you are saying: (1) you want to have a party and (2) you don't know how to get started at this point."

Example 3: "You said at least three key things about yourself, David, as you were talking—you like to play baseball and you want to go out for the team, but your parents aren't sure you should play."

Clarifying and Summarizing Ideas

Activity 3.2

Sit in a circle with other students. Someone volunteers and briefly describes something that happened at home or at school. The *persons sitting next to the volunteer clarify or summarize what was heard— first the person on the right and then the person on the left.*

Someone else then volunteers to tell something. The persons sitting to the right and left summarize or clarify the ideas. Go around the group until each person has had a chance to practice. If someone in the group is unable to clarify or summarize, then the volunteer can help with some important words or ideas.

Focus on the Person's Feelings

Feeling words are important to a friendly helper. They show understanding and acceptance. You will want to use them in your talk with others. When people hear you say something about their feelings, they will feel closer to you. They will learn that you are understanding of them. Sadly, not many people listen for feelings or talk about them. This is something all of us need to practice more. It is a skill that effective facilitators need.

You have already read about feelings and feeling words (Chapter II). You know now that people always talk with emotion (unpleasant and pleasant feelings). Some feelings are stronger than others. They are easy to identify. Other feelings are often there too. But you must listen carefully for them. You will also want to watch for them as they show up in a person's actions.

After you hear or see a feeling (or some feelings) that a person is having, what do you do next? How can you tell the person that you understand?

Making Helpful Responses

Kelly was hoping to be elected by his classmates to the student council. But, when the votes were counted, Kelly was not elected. After class, Kelly looked unhappy. Look at these examples. Each of them shows that Kelly's "disappointment" is understood.

Example 1: "Kelly, you feel disappointed."

Example 2: "Kelly, you are disappointed."

Example 3: "Kelly, it's disappointing to you."

Can you think of any other ways to arrange the words to tell Kelly that you hear disappointment? No matter how the words might be arranged, the most important part of your statement would be the word "disappointment." Or, you may want to use another word like disappointment, such as "discouraged," "sad," or "let down."

All of these words show that you understand Kelly's unpleasant feeling. If you are wrong, he will correct you. Then, you will understand better. If you are on target, then he will feel understood. He will know that you are really listening to him.

Here is another case. It is the story of a young girl who is having problems with her friends. They sometimes get along well with each other. At other times, they argue and say things that hurt each other's feelings.

On this day, Claudette thinks that the other girls (Wendy, Camilla and Janice) are talking about her. She is sure that Janice is trying to get the other girls not to like her. Imagine that Claudette has decided to talk with you about her problem with Janice. Here is how she begins:

Claudette: That Janice is mean. She's a bad one. She's always trying to get my friends away from me. Like today, there she is telling lies about me—like I told stories about Wendy and Camilla being stuck-up, and things like that. . . . Well, it just isn't true! Why does Janice do things like that? I didn't ever do anything to her. I just hate her and hope that she gets what's coming to her one of these days!

That's a lot of words from Claudette. She has said a lot to you. Did you hear pleasant or unpleasant feelings, or both? What are some words that might tell what Claudette was feeling? She seems to have many feelings. (See Table 1 in Chapter II if it can help).

Now, it's your turn to respond. What will you say? You could ask her some questions. Or, you could try to summarize or clarify her main ideas about Janice. However, this time think of a feeling-focused response. *Write* some statements below that tell the feelings and show that you understand.

A possible response:

_____

_____

_____

Another possible response:

_____

_____

_____

Another possible response:

_____

_____

_____

Now, look at your responses. *Underline* the feeling word that you used in each response.

As you practice responding to feelings, it might be helpful to remember that this is a skill that needs a lot of practice. More and more people are learning to hear feelings and to speak up about them. Yet, some people—including many adults—are still just learning about this skill. You might find it difficult at first, but with practice, it will get easier and you will feel more at ease.

Feeling-Focused Responses

Activity 3.3

Sit in a circle with other students. Someone volunteers and tells something that happend at home or at school. The persons sitting next to the volunteer respond to the feelings that were heard — first the person on the right, then the person on the left.

If it helps, start by deciding if the feelings were unpleasant, pleasant, or both. Someone else then volunteers to tell something. The persons sitting to the right and left make their feeling-focused responses. After everyone has had a turn, talk about the responses.

Making Helpful Responses

Following Charlie's Talk

Activity 3.4

Charlie is talking to a facilitator about something that is important to him. Here are some responses that were given to him.

1. "It's going to be your favorite color — red."

2. "How will you earn the money to buy it?"

3. "It's exciting to think about it."

4. "Have your ever had one before?"

5. "It was discouraging to see the price tag."

6. "Let me see, first you are going to look around some more and then you are going to decide."

Can you identify each of the helping statements that were made to Charlie?

What do you think is important to him?

Becoming a Friendly Helper

Connect the dots below by following the *odd numbers only.* You will get a picture of what Charlie talked about.

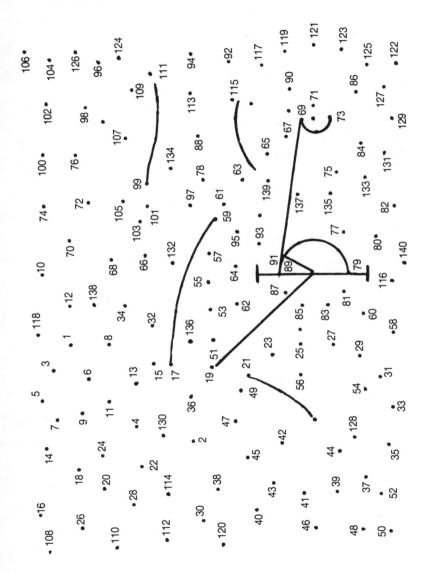

Summary

There are many things that you can do and say when trying to be a friendly helper. Some are more helpful than others. Three very helpful responses are:

1. Ask Open Questions
2. Clarify and Summarize Ideas
3. Make Feeling-Focused Statements

When you use these three responses, the persons you are helping can then think more about their ideas and feelings. You will be seen as a careful listener. You will show that you care and that you are trying to understand. What you say can make you a friendly helper.

Chapter IV

Helping Solve Problems

Deborah was a fifth grade student who rode the bus to school. She liked sitting with her friends and talking with them about all sorts of things. The bus ride was okay, except for one thing. Deborah's little sister, who was in the first grade, also rode the bus and often got into trouble with the bus driver.

Deborah's mother said, "Now, you look out for her. She's your sister and you take care of her. Don't let her bother the other children. Sit with her and make her keep her hands to herself. That's not much to ask, is it?"

So, each day Deborah had to watch after her little sister, who wouldn't listen to Deborah. In the eyes of her sister, Deborah was "bossy" and "mean." Deborah's friends still sat together and talked about their interests. Feeling left out and angry, Deborah often spoke sharply to her sister. Other times she sat quietly, staring out of the window.

Deborah had a problem. She had some unpleasant feelings. What could she do? What would you do?

Problems, Problems, Problems!

A problem is something that happens which makes you "stirred up" with unpleasant feelings. It is something that you must work on before you can feel "settled" or easy again.

Problems are challenges. While some are more serious than others, problems are a part of everyday living. Some last longer than others and demand more attention. Some problems seem like they will never end, while others are solved quickly. However, all of us can learn to solve problems better. Problem-solving is an important skill for student facilitators.

Students Have Problems Too

Activity 4.1

Here are some problems that some students say that they have had. Read the problems. Put an "X" in front of those that you, or students you know, have had.

_____1. I am having trouble understanding and learning my math.

_____2. I don't want to read out loud to the class.

_____3. I just can't seem to get along with teachers.

_____4. I have trouble getting along with my brothers and sisters.

_____5. I have difficulty following our family rules.

_____6. I have to take care of someone who is sick.

_____7. I have trouble making new friends.

_____8. I like a girl, but she doesn't like me.

_____9. My grandfather smokes too much.

_____10. My mother nags me about my grades.

_____11. My dad works too much. He thinks we need things, but I want him to spend more time with me.

_____12. I am overweight.

_____13. I hate tests.

_____14. I don't like the idea of getting old.

_____15. I don't like the darkness in my room at night.

Who Has Problems?

Everyone has problems sometimes. It is natural for people of all ages to be concerned about things and other people. Even little children have problems which they try to work out. For example, whenam's baby brother is hungry, he has a problem. He wants food and cries to let others know that he is hungry. When his mother feeds him his problem is over—for awhile.

As children grow older, mothers and fathers aren't always around to help fix things. For example:

Jimmy, a second grade student, was scared to go to school. He was afraid that some big kids would pick on him. He had to decide what to do. At first, Jimmy cried and said he was sick. He wanted to stay home from school, but he had to go to school anyway. Jimmy was "stirred up." He felt scared and had trouble deciding what to do next.

Helping Solve Problems

Some people always seem to be happy. They don't look like they have any problems. When we see them, they may be wearing a friendly smile. However, even these "happy people" have their share of problems, too. Some hide stirred up feelings behind their smiles because they don't want anyone to know about their problems. They are afraid nobody will understand. For example:

Tom is an excellent student. He usually had all As on his report card. On his last card he received three Bs. He knew that he had not studied as much as before. What would his parents think? He knew that his teacher was disappointed in him. Some of his classmates wished they had his "problem." They didn't see why he was so upset.

Tom thought no one would understand. He put on a smile and pretended that his grades didn't bother him. He laughed and said, "Who cares? I don't." Tom seemed happy enough, but he really wasn't.

Becoming a Friendly Helper

Adults have problems, too. Think of a time when your teachers were stirred up with emotion. What were they feeling? Can you think of some feeling words that would describe what was happening inside them? Who could they talk with about their problem? Could they talk with you?

Our president, governors, and other leaders face many problems in government. The problems are complex and they need careful listeners. To help them, assistants collect information and listen to their ideas. Talking with others helps settle problems. With this kind of help, our leaders can find the best solutions.

Some presidents also faced difficult problems in their personal lives. President Lincoln's mother died when he was nine years old. He also had some business failures later in life. Write two feeling words on the lines below that describe how President Lincoln might have felt on these occasions. Use Table 1 in Chapter II if it will help.

_____

_____

President Roosevelt's legs were paralyzed from the disease polio. He needed a wheelchair and special braces. Write two feeling words on the lines below that decribe how he might have felt.

_____

_____

These presidents had problems, but they learned to overcome them. Who helped them with their personal problems? History books don't often report the work of some friendly helpers.

A Problem-Solving Model

Some problems are easy to solve. We seem to know just what to do. However, at other times problems are more difficult and take more effort. These problems need special attention.

When a difficult problem arises, some people worry so much that they rush into a quick solution. However, the first and easiest answer is not always the best. Sometimes quick decisions are regretted later.

On the other hand, other people worry so much that they delay making a decision. They let their problems go on for too long of time and are unhappy.

No one has discovered a sure way of solving everyone's problems. There seem to be no set rules for finding a best solution. There are no sure answers to people's problems. What, then, are you to do when helping others?

You can learn a five-step problem-solving model that other student facilitators have found useful. It can help you and someone else to make decisions when problems are difficult.

The Model: Five Important Questions

When people talk with you about their problems, focus on their feelings and ideas. As a friendly helper, help them talk about themselves. This takes careful attention and your best listening skills. You can also guide them through some problem-solving steps that might be thought of as *five important questions.* Look at these steps and questions:

Step 1: What is the problem?

Step 2: What have you tried?

Step 3: What else could you do and what would happen?

Step 4: What's your next step?

Step 5: How did it go?

Step 1: "What is the problem?"

In this first step, the person talks about a situation. As you have learned, listen carefully and use open questions. Clarify ideas and make feeling-focused responses. Don't rush. Let the person tell you about the situation. When you think you understand what the problem is, try summarizing it in a few words.

The Case of Kevin: Kevin liked baseball. He was a good fielder and loved to bat. His parents worried about his grades. He had not done well in spelling or math. They told him that he had to do better on his next report card, or he would not be able to play baseball.

Kevin studied very hard for two weeks. But, there was little improvement on his test scores. He thought about giving up, but he wanted very much to play baseball. One day he tore up a test and threw it in the wastebasket on his way out of the classroom. He was angry.

Let's pretend that Kevin wanted your help with his problem. After you both find a place to be alone, he begins to tell you about it.

Kevin: Nothing I do turns out right. I tried and tried, but it didn't do any good.

Your response: (Write a response.)

_____

_____

_____

Kevin: I really want to play baseball, but I can't get those dumb spelling and math tests.

Your response:

_____

_____

_____

Kevin: See, my parents told me that if I don't do better in spelling and math, I can't play baseball this summer.

Your response:

_____

_____

_____

Kevin: Yeah, and I'd rather play baseball than do that dumb old math stuff, anyway.

Your response:

_____

_____

_____

Kevin: I tried real hard this time. I studied and studied, but I still didn't do better on today's tests. I don't know what to do.

Your response:

_____

_____

_____

Did you use facilitative responses? Did you focus on Kevin's feelings, clarify or summarize his ideas and ask him questions? What, then, is Kevin's problem? Complete the following response.

"Kevin, it seems that your problem is _____

_____."

Step 2: "What have you tried?"

After you help clarify the problem, you can ask a person this question: *"What have you tried?"* This second question will help you both think about what's been done to this point. Then, together you can explore what has been working and what has not. Remember, the person will also be sharing some important feelings during this step too. Be sure to respond to some of them.

Let's continue to help Kevin by writing some more helpful responses. You begin this step by asking him: "What have you tried so far, Kevin?"

Kevin: Well, I studied every night after dinner this week. I paid real close attention in class and I did all the homework.

Your response: What else have you done, Kevin?

Kevin: I also tried not to watch TV until I got my homework done. Sometimes that worked and sometimes it didn't.

Your response: _____

_____

People may tell you many things that they have done. It is still helpful to ask, *"What else have you tried?"* You want them to think about all the ways that they have tried to work out their problem. Sometimes they think of better ideas just from talking about what they have done already. Then, go on to the next step.

Step 3: "What else could you do and what would happen?"

You and Kevin have discussed his problem and what he has done. Now, it is time to "brainstorm" some other possible ideas. You can encourage Kevin to talk more by asking: *"What else could you do?"* This will lead him to think of still other ideas and solutions.

As he talks about each idea, ask: *"What would happen?"* He will then think about the results his actions might have. Every action has some kind of result. Thinking about what he might do and the results of his actions can help Kevin select the best course to follow.

Now, try these with Kevin:

Your response: What else could you do?

Kevin: Well, maybe I could talk to Mr. Kelsey (his teacher) about it.

Your response: What would happen if you do that?

Kevin: He might give me some ideas.

Your response: What else could you do?

Kevin: Well, . . . I could ask my friend, Pete, to help.

Your response: What would happen if you ask Pete?

Kevin: He would probably tell me to do things which would get me into trouble.

Your response: He would have some ideas, but they lead to trouble. Okay, what else could you do?

Kevin: I don't know.

Your response: You can't think of anything else?

Kevin: Hum. . . . No, I can't think of anything.

If you have any ideas that might work, wait until Kevin has finished telling you all his ideas. Then, offer your sug-

gestions. Do you have any for Kevin? If you have, write
them here:

Your response: Well, Kevin, you might _____

_____ .

Step 4: "What's your next Step?"

Now it is time for Kevin to decide what he is going to do.
There might be several ideas from which he could
choose. Ask Kevin: *"What is your next step?* He can think
about it and choose between some of the ideas that have
been discussed. Begin again:

Your response: Kevin, what is your next step?

Kevin: I don't know. Maybe I'll go talk to Mr. Kelsey.
Maybe he can give me some help. Besides, then
maybe he'll think of something if he knows what's
happening to me.

Your response: _____

_____

Kevin: It's kind of scary though.

Your response: _____

_____

Kevin: Maybe if I can get Jerry to go with me, it would be
easier.

Your response: _____

_____

Kevin: Yep, that's what I'm going to have to do.

Your response: *When* are you going to do it?

Kevin: Oh. . . I guess at noon tomorrow. He usually eats
alone in his room and then nobody would be
around to bother us.

Step 5: "How did it go?"

The last important part of the problem-solving model is to follow-up. Let the person talk about how things turned out. *How did it go?* This final step will show that you really care about the person.

Kevin might enjoy talking with you again about the meeting with his teacher. No matter what happens, he may want to think about the situation some more. He may need some more help to think about the results and about another plan.

Some problem-solving can take place in one or two brief meetings. Other problems take more time. Some times several meetings are needed before things are settled.

Student facilitators help people move toward their goals. They help them take the next steps that are needed to solve a problem. If a person still has a problem, after going through the five steps try again. If you are unsure of what you should do next, talk with the school counselor. You can also suggest that your friend talk with someone who has more experience. You might be of more help at a later time.

Summary

There are a lot of ways to solve a problem. Some are better than others. The best problem-solvers usually have a plan which they can use. It makes things go easier.

This chapter described five steps and questions that you can use when helping others. When you are helping people with their problems, use these steps:

Step 1: What is the problem?

Step 2: What have you tried?

Step 3: What else could you do and what would happen?

Step 4: What is your next step?

Step 5: How did it go?

A Problem-Solving Journey

Activity 4.2

Beth has a problem. She is new to school and tells you that she doesn't have any friends. You can lead her through the five problem-solving steps. Start at the beginning and follow the maze, leading her through the steps, until you reach the end.

Start Here

What is the problem?

What have you tried?

What else could you do? What would Happen?

Finish ☆

How did it go?

What is your next step?

Becoming a Friendly Helper

Chapter V

Giving Feedback

People with problems want to talk with a person who is caring, accepting, understanding, and trustworthy. You can be such a person by asking open questions, clarifying and summarizing ideas, and responding to feelings. These three kinds of responses can be helpful as you guide someone through the problem-solving model.

If you are a careful listener and have some helpful suggestions, you can be a valuable friend to someone who is having problems. But, most friends want to know more about what you are feeling and thinking about them. They want to know what reactions you are having to them. How do you see them? They will sometimes want some *feedback.*

Feedback is a term that comes from science. Scientists need feedback or information from machines to tell them when things are on or off target. They must have some device that tells them when to make corrections in their work. In this sense, feedback tells them whether they are right or wrong.

Human beings are too complex to give feedback like a machine or a computer. Everyone is different and not everyone sees things the same way. Some people do things the same. Others do them differently. Yet, all may achieve the same good results. Exact directions for living life and making decisions are almost impossible. Instead, we rely on our best judgment and feedback from others to make choices and decisions.

A Feedback Model

How can you give others feedback? What can you do to help others learn more about your reactions to them? This chapter has a three-part model that can be used with students and adults. The three parts are not a final answer for telling others what you think and feel about them. But, they are a guide that can help you organize your thoughts, tell what you've seen or heard, and what you are feeling. This model helps you tune-in to yourself and speak up.

Part 1: Be Specific About What You See and Hear.

If you are going to give someone feedback, you must be aware of what that person is doing. Pay close attention. Listen not only to the person's words but how the words are said. The eyes, mouth, and body position can be clues to what the person is feeling. Use all the information you can to form your ideas.

A person also may trigger feelings in you. Then, you may want to tell the person somthing. In that case, describe what you see and hear, or what has happened. Be specific. Give an example, if you can.

Darrell watched his little brother open a birthday gift that he had given him. His brother was excited. His eyes got big and he had a wide smile. "Oh boy—it's just what I wanted—thanks a lot, thanks a lot!"

Even though you were not there, can you imagine what Darrell's little brother was doing? If it helps, close your eyes and picture in your mind someone—like Darrell's brother—opening a gift. The person finds just what was wanted. Can you imagine it?

Think of the many things that Darrell might notice about his little brother—his actions and his words. Being a careful observer and getting a picture is one of the first things you must do, if you are going to tell others about themselves. The more you can tell what you saw and heard, the better you will be in giving feedback.

Part 2: Tell What You Are Feeling.

After you have told a person what you have noticed, it is time to tune-in to yourself. Be aware of what you are feeling. Are you having unpleasant feelings or pleasant feelings? If it helps, use your list of feeling words. Find one word that best describes what you are feeling inside. Your feeling is the impact or effect that the person is having on you. It is your reaction to them. Now, speak up. *Let the person know how that person has made you feel.*

You might feel differently from time to time about things that people do. In one situation you might have different feelings than in another. For example, if you received a gift you might feel happy and excited. At another time, you might be disappointed or sad if it is less than what you expected.

Your feelings can change from time to time. Someone might tell you about something that they have done. It may make you feel happy to hear about it. But, as the person talks more, you might begin to feel a little jealous or envious. You may feel both pleasant and unpleasant feelings.

The most important part of giving feedback is to tell the person what you are feeling.

Part 3: Tell What Your Feelings Make You Want To Do.

Our feelings influence our actions. For example, when you are happy and having fun, you smile and laugh more than at other times. When you are sad and worried, you frown and are less active than at other times. When you are angry, your voice may get louder. You might even say some sharp and hurting words. When you are thankful, you might tell people how much you like what they did You might also say that it makes you want to be around them more.

Feelings can be expressed in many ways. Some ways are better than others. For instance, if you have some warm and caring feelings about your mother, you might:

1. Touch her softly on the arm and smile at her; or

2. compliment her for something that she has done; or

3. make her a special thank you card; or

4. offer to help with something she is doing; or

5. tell others about how much you care about her; or

6. tell her how special she is to you.

What else can you think of? There are so many things you could do. What you do depends upon what you are feeling. What do some of your feelings make you want to do? What part do your feelings play in what you do with others?

This third step in giving facilitative feedback will help others learn more about the impact that they have on you. It can also help you learn more about yourself.

Using the Feedback Model

Look at the cases below. They can help you learn more about feedback. Can you find the three parts in the first case? Put a single line under part one, a double line under part two, and three lines under part three.

Case 1: "Donna, you asked Alex if he would try the game again, even though he lost, I was glad. I just wanted to tell you that before we got started in our work."

Let's try another one. This time, however, the order of the three parts have been changed. See if you can find each part by putting a single line under part one, a double line under part two, and three lines under part three.

Case 2: "Ronnie, I'm really excited right now. I want to be a student facilitator because I heard you talk about it."

You may want to practice using the three steps or parts in the order that they were first discussed in this chapter. But, you can mix the order, if you wish. Remember to be specific about what the person does, what you are feeling, and what you want to do.

Family Feedback

Okay, it's time for you to put together some feedback statements of your own. Begin by thinking of someone in your family. It might be either your mother or your father, or someone with whom you are living.

Looking for Part 1. Think of a time when you liked being with this person. That is, think of when you had a pleasant experience with this person. Picture it in your mind. Now, write in a sentence or two, what the person did. __

_____

_____

_____

Looking for Part 2. Next, think about what pleasant feelings you had at that time. Write some of those pleasant feeling words here:

_____

_____

_____

Looking for Part 3. Think about what those feelings made you want to do. They might have made you want to do many things. List some of them here:

_____

_____

_____

Putting the Parts Together. Look back at what you have written. You now have enough information for all the parts of the feedback model. Put all three parts together by picking the words you want to use. Write a feedback response to that person here:

(name) _____ , when you _____

_____

_____

_____ .

Now, put a single line under part one (the person's actions), a double line under part two (your feelings), and three lines under part three (what you want to do). Finally, circle the feeling word or words you used.

Some Feedback to Others

Activity 5.1

Practice giving some feedback by writing some examples of your own on a piece of paper. Think of people who you would like to give some feedback. Write two or three examples of feedback that you could give these people.

After you have written the examples, can you identify the three parts of the feedback model?

Feedback to Rod

Here are some more examples of when two people (Clara and Don) gave feedback to a boy named Rod at different times.

Clara: Hey, Rod, when you invited me to go to your house on Saturday, it sure made me happy. I just wanted you to know that I am looking forward to it and can hardly wait.

Don: I was really glad, Rod, when you said "hello" to me that first day at school. It made me want to thank you for being so friendly.

Clara: Rod, when you said that I should mind my own business, I really got mad. It made me want to tell you that you're not the only one who cares.

Don: I'm kind of sad right now, Rod. When you told me that I'd hurt your feelings because I teased you about your hair, I started thinking more about what I said. I'm sorry.

What is the difference between the first two examples and the last two examples? In the first two examples, Clara and Don are telling Rod about their *pleasant feelings.* These pleasant feelings came from something that he did. In the last two examples, they are sharing some of their *unpleasant feelings* about something he did. In all the examples, however, Clara and Don are using the three parts of the feedback model.

Complimenting and Confronting Others

We can tune-in to the pleasant feelings we have about what others have done. When we describe these feelings to them, we are *complimenting* them. We are being positive. We are saying something that can cause some pleasant feelings in them.

However, when we tune-in to our unpleasant feelings about what others do, and tell them, we are *confronting* them. There are times to compliment and times to confront. We must learn to do both if we are going to be a real friend and true to ourselves.

Some students don't know what to do with their unpleasant feelings. If they are mad, for example, they might throw things or hit people. They don't know how to talk their problems out. They don't know how to tell their feelings. So, they "act out" to show how they feel and this can cause problems for others.

Learning to tell about your unpleasant feelings can be a very valuable tool. Try to avoid giving advice and telling all of your unpleasant feelings. Focus on those that are building up and really bothering you.

You can help others talk with you about the situation or problem. Be a careful listener. You could also build up some caring, acceptance, understanding, and trust before you confront. Take time to listen and let them talk about what is on their minds. Then, your ideas are much more likely to be heard when it is your turn to talk.

Think of someone whom you would like to confront. What has the person done to cause you some unpleasant feelings? What are your feelings? What do those feelings make you want to do? Now, can you think of something else to talk about with this person? Talk with them. After listening, do you still want to confront them? This is a useful test to give yourself before you confront anyone.

Think of some people that you would like to compliment? What have they have done to cause you some pleasant feelings? What do those pleasant feelings make you want to do? Don't delay. Seek out some of those persons soon. When the time is right, tell them some of your thoughts and feelings using the feedback model. You will be surprised how pleasant it will be for you and the other persons.

Time for Another Compliment

Activity 5.2

Think of another person that you would like to compliment. Using the feedback model, give the person a compliment. Try to use all three parts of the model, mixing the order as you wish.

Draw a picture telling about that time. Under the picture, write what you said to the person.

Summary

Your friends often want to know what you think about them. They want to know what kind of impact they are having on you. With the help of a three-part feedback model, you can either compliment or confront them. To give effective feedback you will want to:

Part 1: Be specific about what you see and hear.

Part 2: Tell what you are feeling (pleasant or unpleasant, or both).

Part 3: Tell what your feelings make you want to do.

The feedback model, and the other helping responses you learned earlier, are skills need by friendly helpers.

Chapter VI

Looking At Yourself and Others

Open your left hand. Place it in front of you so that you can see it. Reach out with your other hand. Shake hands and smile! Say "hello" to a very special friend—you!

As a student facilitator, you will be a friend to many people. Because of the skills that you have learned and practiced, others will value your friendship. They will like being around you. They will enjoy having you as a friend.

Friends are very important. Some people spend a life time looking for friends and worrying whether or not they have enough friends. It seems that when we have friends, then we like ourselves better and enjoy life more. Can you ever have too many friends? Are some friends closer to you than others? Who is your best friend?

Close friends get more of our attention than others. We get to know them better and take more interest in them. We give them more of our time. We expect them to ask us for help when they need it. We are close, but not so close that we give them all our attention, time and energy. They are not the only people we care about, accept and trust. They are important to us, but so are other people.

One of the best friends that you will ever have is very close to you right now. Do you know who it is? You just shook hands and said hello to your closest friend. That's right—it's you! You are your own best friend! How much do you really know about yourself? What kind of a friend are you to yourself?

While you may have many friends, no one will know you as well as you know yourself. You will share ideas and feelings with others. You will also have many ideas and feelings that you are unable or don't want to talk about.

Sometimes you cannot share them because there is not enough time, the place is not right, or some situations prevent it. At other times, you will have private thoughts and feelings that you want to keep to yourself. This is why you must be a good friend to yourself. Listen carefully to your inner thoughts and feelings. You, too, will find it helpful to explore your ideas.

Imagine that you are in a very difficult situation. You're feeling unsure of yourself. What kind of thoughts might go through your mind? You might ask yourself questions such as: "What am I doing here?" or, "What should I do now?" You might even give some directions to yourself: "I really need to think about this more." Or, "I'd better do something, right away!" Then there are times when you may talk with yourself and reach some conclusions: "Hey, that was a pretty good idea." "That's neat!" "Things are going well for me today!" Or, "That's one of the dumbest things I've ever done."

Becoming a Friendly Helper

This kind of "inner talk" with yourself can be valuable. It helps you to get a better understanding of yourself and to think things through. On the other hand, if you spend too much time wondering about yourself, then you may cause yourself even more problems. Thinking only of yourself—to be totally self-centered—can make you blind to the world around you.

Many people don't really know themselves. They are so busy thinking about other things. They fail to realize how special they are. It takes time to know one's self. But, self-understanding is a gift that we can give ourselves. It makes life more fun and interesting. Without self-understanding, persons are limited in what they can do. With self-understanding, a person can solve problems and facilitate others better.

In this chapter you will learn more about yourself. You will also learn how to help others take a closer look at themselves.

Here are some questions that you can probably answer very easily. Write an answer to each one.

1. What is the color of your hair? _____

2. Are you left-handed or right-handed? _____

3. Where do you live? _____

4. What school do you attend? _____

Here are some other questions that may need more thought. Now, answer these questions.

1. What is your favorite vacation place? _____

2. What animal would you like most to have as a pet? _

_____

3. What is your least favorite color? _____

4. Who do you like to play with the most? _____

There are still other questions that you might ask yourself. They may take even more time because you must explore your thoughts and feelings to find answers. Try these:

1. You are going to another planet to live for the rest of your life. You can only take three things, besides your family. What would they be?

   _____

   _____

   _____

2. What is one thing that would make the world better?

   _____

3. Who do you most want to be like?

   _____

4. What are two things you would like to change about yourself?

   (a) _____

   (b) _____

Answering questions about yourself can be interesting and fun. Sometimes, however, it's puzzling or confusing. Yet, as you ask yourself questions and seek answers, self-understanding grows.

Your Self-Image

Your self-image is the picture that you have of yourself. It is how you have come to see yourself.

Do you see yourself as a happy person? Do you think that you are too heavy or too thin? Do you think that you are strong or weak? The answers to these questions, and others like them, can help you learn more about your self-image.

Your self-image affects the way you do things. You might believe that you are not very good at something. This belief can discourage you from trying. It could even make you give up easily.

Sally was a sixth grade student who didn't like spelling. One day her friend asked why she wasn't studying for a spelling test. Sally said, "It won't do any good, anyway." Sally thought she was going to fail, even if she studied. When the teacher finally gave the test, she did not do well. After class, Sally told her friend, "See, I told you. I'm a poor speller. I just can't get those words right."

The thoughts we have about ourselves can influence our efforts. How did Sally's thoughts affect her test results? If she saw herself positively, could she do better?

When Jerome looked in a mirror, he felt sad. He was shorter and thinner than the other boys in his class and he didn't like it. He worried about his strength. His father asked him if he wanted to join the community Boy's Club and play on a team. Jerome wanted to play more sports and compete with the other boys. But, he didn't like what he saw when he looked in the mirror.

What kind of thoughts do you think Jerome is having about his "self?" How might Jerome's self-image affect his decisions? Write some of your ideas here:

_____

_____

_____

_____

What can you do to discover more about your self-image? How can you help others think more about themselves? Where do you begin? There are at least four areas where you can start your search of "self."

(1) physical self,

(2) beliefs and attitudes,

(3) skills and abilities,

(4) self with others.

Your Physical Self

No two people look exactly the same. Even identical twins have their differences, if you look closely. It would be a strange world if we all looked alike. Our differences make life more interesting. Most important, they also make each of us unique and special.

Some people don't like how they look and how they are different. Others like themselves better but can still find something about their physical self that they would like to change. Still others don't care. Yet, how we see our physical self can influence what happens in our lives.

Becky was a fourth grade girl who knew that her parents made less money than others. Her family had fewer things, including money for nice clothes. Becky was ashamed of what she wore and thought that she wasn't very pretty.

Becky often wore the same two dresses to school. Her hair was usually tangled and dull. It hung down over her eyes and looked uncared for. Her hands were often dirty. But, behind her unkept appearance, Becky had a nice smile. When she smiled and stood up straight, her eyes were bright and friendly.

She had some private talks with a "friendly helper" who noticed her. At one point, the facilitator helped her think more about her appearance and what others might notice most about her. "Becky, when I see you at school and see that you haven't brushed your hair, it makes me wonder. I ask myself, "Why doesn't she care about herself more?"

This feedback caught Becky by surprise. She had taken little time to do anything about her appearance. She was too busy feeling sad for herself. Becky thought that no one noticed or cared.

One day, Becky decided to get up early and wash her hair. She brushed it until it was shiny and free of tangles. She also washed her face and hands. It was refreshing to get the sleep out of her eyes and feel her clean skin. She wondered if anyone would notice. Most important, she felt better about herself.

When she arrived at school, her teacher saw the change at once. "Hi, Becky, did your mother do your hair this morning? It looks so pretty." Becky felt herself smile and stand taller. She was suddenly less afraid to look at others in the class. She felt proud of herself. Taking better care of her physical self seemed more important. Though she didn't have many clothes, she learned that she could still do things to help her look and feel better.

Some students worry that they are too short. Others worry that they are too tall. Some don't like the way they look at all and fear that others will make fun of them. These students have a difficult time accepting their physical selves.

Whether we like it or not, all of us are given certain physical traits by our parents. These traits are passed down from one generation to another. We must learn to accept the parts of the physical self that cannot be changed. This includes color of skin, eyes, and hair. We must also accept the size of our noses, feet, hands, and legs. Yet, given what we are born with, there are still some things that we can change.

John, a friend of Becky's, was shorter than other boys his age. But, he lifted weights and exercised to build up his strength. Later other boys learned to respect him for both his size and strength. Becky, of course, learned that she felt prettier when she took time to groom herself.

Are there some things about your appearance that you don't like? Which ones would you change if you could? Which ones can you change? Which ones must you learn to live with and accept as part of who you are? Your attitudes about your physical self influence the way you are around others and the confidence you have in yourself.

Your Beliefs and Attitudes

What are some things that you believe are true about life? About people? About school? About the future? You already have beliefs and attitudes that influence your decisions and actions. You will keep some of these forever. Others will change as you grow older. What beliefs and attitudes are most important to you now?

All of us learn things from others about life. We learn a lot from our families. They teach us to think about ourselves. We also learn from our teachers and friends. They have their own beliefs about what is right and wrong and what is best for them. Our beliefs also come from television, books, newspapers, churches and synagogues, and from many other places. Our attitudes and beliefs influence what we do.

Can a person disagree with your beliefs and still be your friend?

Think more about your beliefs and attitudes. This will help you to relax and to listen better to others. It also helps you to understand other points of view.

You can be a good listener even though you disagree. Student facilitators help others explore ideas and feelings. They try not to tell others what they should believe. They help individuals make their own decisions.

Becoming a Friendly Helper

Your Skills and Abilities

All of us are skillful at some things and not so skillful at others. We all have skills. We are proud of some and would like to improve others.

It also seems that some people have more natural ability to do things than others. Yet, all of us can develop our skills and abilities more. We can all be successful at some things.

Your skills and abilities influence the way you feel and act. When you have mastered the skills in this book, you will feel better about helping others. You will have more confidence in your ability.

Sometimes it is helpful to keep your personal strengths and limits in mind. For example:

> Juan was a new student from Argentina. When the boys met after school to play football, he stood on the sidelines and watched curiously. This was a different kind of game than he had played before. Football in Argentina was not the same. It was more like the sport of soccer and Juan had learned some different skills. He was skilled at using his feet and head rather than his hands. Juan wasn't even sure of the game rules.

Later the boys asked Juan to play. Juan felt a little scared and unsure. He couldn't pass the ball very well and usually fumbled it when it was passed to him. He was embarrassed. He wondered if he should continue playing. However, when it came time to punt the football, Juan's kicking skill really showed. The ball went high and sailed through the air. The other boys were amazed at how far he kicked the ball. This gave Juan more confidence. It helped him to relax and enjoy the game more.

He had a skill that others could learn from him. But, he also knew that he had to learn some other skills.

Like Juan, you do some things well. There are also some skills and abilities that you will want to improve. Get involved and practice.

Becoming a Friendly Helper

Your Self With Others

We know that other people influence the way we think about ourselves and the things we do. When we tell a funny story, people might laugh and smile with us. This tells us that what we did was fun for them. It also tells us that we can be funny at times. Yet, when we say other things, people might frown or look worried. This tells us that we are doing something that concerns them. What they do and say can make us wonder about ourselves. We may even stop doing whatever they frowned upon.

How do others see you? Are you the same around everyone? Do you act the same with your teachers as you do with your friends? What about your actions with people who are younger than you?

Sandra was a friendly helper. She and her friends used this book to learn more about themselves. In a group activity, she described how her classmates might see her. She wrote: (1) helpful, (2) smart, and (3) funny, at times.

Then she wrote what her teacher might say about her. The words were: (1) nice, (2) helpful, and (3) talks a lot.

How are the two lists similar? Different? Which words are positive? Negative? If she wanted to change these views, what could she do?

What words would you write in this activity? How do your classmates see you? What do you do that makes them think of you this way? What about your teachers?

Like Sandra, it may be worth your time to think more about how you are with others.

Becoming a Friendly Helper

Summary

You will have many thoughts about yourself. Your inner talk can help you think things through. However, you will also want to talk with others in order to learn more about yourself. Knowing about self lets you solve personal problems and facilitate others better.

One way to gain more self understanding is to know more about your self-image. Your self-image is the picture that you have of yourself. There are at least four ways you can bring your self-picture into focus:

1. Study your physical self. (What are your physical traits?)

2. Study your beliefs and attitudes. (What do you believe?)

3. Study your skills and abilities. (What can you do?)

4. Study how you are with others. How do you act with others? How do they act with you/)

Learning to be a student facilitator can be fun. You learn skills that help others, but you also learn more about yourself.

Looking at Your Self-Image

Activity 6.1

For each of the statements, circle the:

"SD" if you strongly disagree.

"D"   if you disagree.

"U"   if you are undecided.

"A"   if you agree.

"SA" if you strongly agree.

Your Physical Self

SD D U A SA   1. I like the color of my eyes.

SD D U A SA   2. I am strong.

SD D U A SA   3. I like my hair.

SD D U A SA   4. I am tall enough for my age.

SD D U A SA   5. I am at a good weight for my height.

SD D U A SA   6. I wash my hands often enough.

SD D U A SA   7. I like my hair.

SD D U A SA   8. I look okay.

Your Skills and Abilities

SD D U A SA   1. I am smart.

SD D U A SA   2. I have good ideas.

SD D U A SA   3. I have good study habits.

SD D U A SA   4. I am a careful listener.

SD D U A SA   5. I can read well.

SD D U A SA   6. I am good in arithmetic.

SD D U A SA   7. I am good in sports.

SD D U A SA   8. I am good in music.

Your Beliefs and Attitudes

SD D U A SA   1. I would rather watch television than play a game with a friend.

SD D U A SA   2. I would rather live in a big city than in a small town.

SD D U A SA   3. Money is the most important thing in life.

SD D U A SA   4. It is okay for boys to cry.

SD D U A SA   5. Religion is important to me.

SD D U A SA   6. Sometimes telling a lie is okay.

SD D U A SA   7. Reading and arithmetic are more important than sports.

SD D U A SA   8. Girls are good athletes.

Yourself with Others

SD D U A SA   1. I make friends easily.

SD D U A SA   2. My friends like my ideas.

SD D U A SA   3. My classmates make fun of me.

SD D U A SA   4. I get picked on by my classmates.

SD D U A SA   5. I have lots of friends.

SD D U A SA   6. My parents are disappointed in me.

SD D U A SA   7. My teacher likes me.

SD D U A SA   8. More people like me than don't like me.

Incomplete Sentences

Activity 6.2

Finish the sentences to tell more about yourself. These can be shared later in the group.

1. I wish my teacher would _____.

2. I would like to change my _____.

3. Others think I'm _____.

4. If others knew me better, they would say_____.

5. Everyone should _____.

6. One of the most important things in life is _____.

7. I wish others would _____.

8. One of my strengths is _____.

9. I can't _____.

10. I would never _____.

11. In the future, I will _____.

12. Something new I'd like to try is _____.

13. If I had more money, I would _____.

14. The color of blue reminds me of _____.

15. One of my worst habits is _____.

16. One thing that would make me happier is _____.

Chapter VII

Becoming a Friendly Helper

You should now have a better idea of what it means to be a student facilitator or friendly helper. The first six chapters of this book gave some important helping skills. You can use these in your work with others. What now?

Your teachers and counselor will have ideas about how you can be a friendly helper in school. You can be a student assistant, tutor, special friend, or small group leader.

Student Assistant. You can work with teachers, counselors, principals, secretaries, and other adults in your school as a student assistant. You might assist a teacher with classroom duties and activities. Or, you might be a member of a safety patrol and assist students to and from school. You could work in the school office and greet visitors or answer the phone. You might help the school counselor welcome new students to your school. Your help will be most valued when you use the ideas in this book.

Tutor. There are students who need extra help in their school work. Some need to "catch up" because they have been absent. Others need to think through some ideas that they are learning. They need coaching and support from someone who understands them. They also need to talk openly and freely about what they are studying. As a tutor you might meet with students your own age or maybe with younger students. You can meet in a small group or work one-to-one. You may do both. As a friendly helper who is a tutor, you will also learn more yourself.

Becoming a Friendly Helper

Special Friend. Some students in your school do not have many friends. They feel left out and lonely. They may act scared or they may be shy. Have you ever noticed someone who stands sadly on the sidelines during recess? You can become a special friend to one or more of these students. You can help them to feel more important, understood, and accepted.

Talking with a special friend like you can be a rewarding experience. It might be just the thing that is needed to help a person gain more confidence. You may never be close friends, but you can share ideas at times. You may even be seen as a big brother or sister or a "buddy."

Small Group Leader. Another role is that of a group leader. Students can benefit from working together in a small group. Group discussions can make school more interesting. There is more chance to share. Some students are shy and need practice in talking before a group. Others are loud and have trouble sitting still. They need practice in listening and working together. Still others want a chance to talk and to hear some reactions. Small group leaders can work with special learning projects, both in and out of the classroom.

One fifth grade friendly helper was the leader of a small group of second grade students. She asked each student to tell about a time when they did something with a friend. After each one talked, she made helping responses that showed careful listening. Everyone had a time to talk and to be heard.

Student facilitators may have different titles, depending on the school. Yet, they all learn some helping skills in training and working with others in projects. They can serve in one or more of the four roles.

Questions Facilitators Have Asked

Being a friendly helper is not always easy. Sometimes things go smoothly. Then again, there will be problem moments. Talk with your trainer about your work. Share your thoughts and feelings with other facilitators. Explore other ways of helping. Here are a few questions that facilitators have thought about.

Who can I help? There are a lot of people, both young and old, who can benefit from your help. Everyone enjoys being with a careful listener. It gives them a chance to talk about ideas and to feel important. They might talk about a problem or about something that is just fun to think about.

There are a lot of young people who would enjoy talking with an older student. Children seldom get much time to talk about themselves. Most people are usually telling them what they should do and think about. You can give them a very special gift by taking some time to listen. You could be with them in a class group, on the playground, or somewhere more private.

Adults can use your help, too. Mothers and fathers, teachers and counselors, also like to talk about their ideas with a good listener.

Am I ready to be a friendly helper? This is a question that you must ask yourself. We hope that this book has been useful. If you are still unsure of yourself or what you might do, talk with your program trainer. But, at this point, you are probably ready. Reach out and be a friendly helper to those around you. They will like you better for it. Your experiences may be remembered for many years to come.

What if a person doesn't want my help? Sometimes people with problems are full of hurt feelings. It is a tough time for them. They may not want to admit that they have unpleasant feelings. They are often unsure of themselves. Be patient. Perhaps it is the wrong time to approach them. Try again some other time. If your caring and interest show, they may want to talk with you later. You may also want to talk with your trainer about the matter.

What if someone wants my help and I can't help? Regardless of how skilled you are, there are some problems that may make you feel uncomfortable. There are limits to what you can do. For example, suppose a group of second graders told you that some "big kids" were taking their lunch bags. As a friendly helper, you can listen and help them think about what they can and can't do. You might also find someone who can give more help than you can. For example, they could talk with a counselor, principal, or teacher. You can be helpful, but friendly helpers sometimes need friendly help too.

You Can Make a Difference

Can you make a difference? It is not possible to list all of the positive things that have been said about student facilitators like you, but here are a few comments:

Jamie (second grade):

I like John. He is my special friend. He talks with me and I talk with him. . . it's fun.

Anthony (third grade):

I like Jim. He is neat. When is he coming back?

Paula (first grade):

I forget her name. . . but she was real nice. We got to talk about how to make friends . . . and stuff like that. I wish we could do more things like that.

Willard (third grade):

Well, you see, I got behind in my school work. I was sick for a long time. Roger explained some of the things I missed. We also talked about some other things too. Catching up was hard work, but he helped me a lot.

Billy (third grade):

The other kids tease me. They call me names. I like it best when Derrick is around and we can talk. He met with all of us and now things are a lot better. But, there is still one guy who I need to talk with Derrick about.

Rosa (kindergarten):

Susan is nice. I wish other big kids were like her.

Parent:

I was really surprised when I heard David talk with his little brother. He was so understanding and helpful. I would never have thought it was possible.

Parent:

Deborah and her friends went into my daughter's second grade class. They took them through some activities. I'm not sure who Deborah is, but my little girl thinks she is wonderful. That's all she's been talking about this week.

Teacher:

I noticed a big change in Ronald since he's been working with Wayne. Ronald is such a lucky boy to have Wayne as a special friend. I wonder if Wayne knows how important he is to Ronald? He may never really know.

Principal:

Student facilitators have made a big difference in our school. They help create a friendly climate. They are also positive examples for others.

Counselor:

Janice doesn't spend much time with Donnie, but that time is important. He's happier, does more school work, and gets along better with others. Janice has really made a difference in Donnie's life.

Congratulations!

If you have carefully studied and practiced the ideas in this book, then you are ready to be a student facilitator.

Here is your *Student Facilitator Merit Award.* Merit awards are only given for special efforts and achievements. You have earned it. This is just the beginning of some very rewarding moments in your life. **You have become a friendly helper!**

Like
Lana

Like
Lana

DANIELLE LEONARD

mosaicPRESS

Library and Archives Canada Cataloguing in Publication

Leonard, Danielle, 1972-, author

    Like Lana / Danielle Leonard.

Issued in print and electronic formats.

ISBN 978-1-77161-333-0 (softcover).--ISBN 978-1-77161-334-7 (HTML).--

ISBN 978-1-77161-335-4 (Kindle).--ISBN 978-1-77161-432-0 (PDF)

    I. Title.

PS8603.I43L55 2019   jC813'.6   C2018-905398-4

                                    C2018-905399-2

Published by Mosaic Press, Oakville, Ontario, Canada, 2019.

MOSAIC PRESS, Publishers
Copyright © Danielle Leonard, 2019

Cover design by Danielle Leonard

ONTARIO ARTS COUNCIL
CONSEIL DES ARTS DE L'ONTARIO
an Ontario government agency
un organisme du gouvernement de l'Ontario

We acknowledge the Ontario Arts Council
for their support of our publishing program

Funded by the Government of Canada
Financé par le gouvernement du Canada

MOSAIC PRESS
1252 Speers Road, Units 1 & 2
Oakville, Ontario L6L 5N9
phone: (905) 825-2130
info@mosaic-press.com

October 28, 2013

When Bad Things Happen to Bad People

This is my last blog post. I need to go away for a long while. And, I didn't want to stop writing without saying good bye. When I first started writing this blog, I thought I could right some wrongs. But, as it turns out, I've done it all wrong. Now, I'm going to tell you why, so read carefully.

I'd always thought the world would finally make sense if only bad things would happen to people who deserve it. Everyone freaks out when bad things happen to good people. We wonder why them?

But what we're really wondering is why can't bad things just happen to the bad people. Like, *somehow* we KNOW who the bad people are. We KNOW who is deserving of bad things. But do any of us really know, with certainty, who the bad ones are?

Maybe it's me. Maybe it's you. Maybe it's your father or mother. Your best friend. Or your worst enemy. There's always the opportunity to see the bad in anyone. It's so easy to do. Too easy, really.

When my life started to fall apart this year, I hated so many people. It was easy to blame everyone else for my pain. But somehow the line between good and bad, victim and villain eventually got blurred. Sure, I started out as the one who everyone hated. So what did I do? I became just like them. A hater.

Now three students are dead. I wish I could say they were the bad ones. That they deserved their fate. But now I see that I'm no different from any of them. Just like each of them, I've done a horrible thing that I cannot undo. But here's the weird part… I don't FEEL like a bad person. I just feel like me.

I wish that I'd realized from the beginning how much we are all struggling together. To find our place in this shitty world called high school. Maybe then nobody would have had to die.

If you've learned anything from my story, I hope it's this… be careful who you judge. Because the harsher you judge, the harder you need to look at the person in the mirror. Next thing you know the bad things that you wish on others, could very well start happening to you.

20 DAYS EARLIER

CHAPTER 1

One is the Loneliest Number

I don't want to get used to this feeling. Of wanting to be invisible, but not wanting it at the same time. But this is nice, slinking along the lockers as the crowd swarms past me. No one turning sideways to notice me. To laugh. Point a finger and say, there's the slut. Which makes it that much more annoying to hear the voice in my head yelling *Look at me! I'm still a person! Look. At. Me.*

Shut up! I mutter back, irritated. Wanting one thing while hoping for the opposite is just plain stupid. Or it's a sign. That I'm fit for the mental ward. I try to shoo the thought away. I'm just lonely.

Lonely.

The thought sits in the hollow of my mind like an old wooden rocking chair. Creaking back and forth driving me just a little more crazy and desperate each day. But there's also the hatred, draped across the chair like an ugly old quilt that's too comfortable to throw out. I wish I could say that I don't want to get used to being hated. After all, it's only been a few weeks since I became the most despised student in school. But there's a weird comfort in the hatred. It gives me something to work with. To build upon. With loneliness, there's nothing.

A group of guys with thick necks sweep past me, punching each other in the shoulders, chests. A fist nicks my shoulder blade. I look up to see who did it, but none of them seem to know, or care, that I'd been hit. I inhale deeply, groaning with my exhalation. A release of something ugly that's accumulated in my chest over the past few weeks. Emotional phlegm.

As the hallway empties, my ears perk at the sound of heels clicking in my direction and my stomach crumples. I hear the familiar high-pitched laugh that curdles in my ears. Do I speed up or wait to let them pass?

"S-s-s-s-slut." The word slithers out. Giving it the venomous quality it so deserves. I cringe, but refuse to face them. I'd know Alysa's voice anywhere. Ten years of gossip-whispering, ice-cream-gorging, inside-joking, boyfriend-bashing years of friendship will do that. I hate her. I hate all of them. The fabbies. It was me who came up with that name to define our exclusive group of girlfriends. Over time, it expanded to include the select few who knew how to dress, how to party and, basically, how to be the envy of everyone else in the grade.

"When are you going to crawl back into the hole you came from?" Alysa asks casually. Like she's talking about our next trip to the shopping mall. I turn to meet her gaze. The fake lashes are extra long today, reaching almost to her eyebrows. Her full lips glint under a fresh coat of pink lip gloss. I try to maintain a stone face as she walks by but the muscles around my eyes and mouth are tensing into something ugly. The f-bomb rolls toward my tongue, but I swallow it. Why give her ammunition to shoot me up with more insults? I've heard my fair share already today. I stop to lean my back against the lockers and stare, my teeth clenching so hard that my jaw aches.

With a smirk and flip of her long black hair, she turns her head and sashays down the hall with BFF Sarah next to her. I watch them until they've been swallowed up by the students gathering around the exit doors, jockeying to be the next to leave.

Three weeks and two days. That's how long I've been the official Sacred Heart High School Bitch target. All because of one photo. I still don't get how it blew up the way it has. I wasn't the first fabbie to let her boyfriend take photos. Not that we openly admitted to doing it, but the assumption was always there. Wasn't it? The way we'd all purse our lips and widen our eyes when teachers warned us of the latest teen headline.

GIRL COMMITS SUICIDE AFTER NUDE PHOTO GOES VIRAL

That would never be one of us, we thought. We prayed. Silently vowing to never do it again. Until it was time to snatch a new boyfriend, or keep the one we had. *We would never do that.* The teacher or cop (after an especially bad headline) would stare hard at each of us until she felt convinced we were speaking the truth. Just a bunch of good kids.

We weren't.

Well, I wasn't. I'd always assumed they weren't either. Maybe I was wrong. I've been realizing lately that I've been wrong about a lot of things in my life. The truth hurts. Yep, cheezy sayings have found new meaning in my life. Here's another one: Life's a bitch and then you die. I'm due to hit the coffin any day now, based on that one.

Still, I'm hopeful that this will all blow over. It can't drag on for much longer. Soon enough, we will all be friends again. Go back to the way it was. At least that's my hope. Delusional, yes, but it's all I've got to get out of bed every morning.

The hallway is almost empty now. Yet, here I am still standing in one place. My eyes fixated on my boots. They are a delicious chocolate brown with copper buckles at the ankles. Mom bought them as a back-to-school surprise gift. Not that I didn't expect to find them on my bed eventually, smelling like fresh, over-priced leather. Every time we'd walked by the store, I'd beg her to buy them. Wearing her down until she was convinced the happiness of my senior year depended on them.

"Everyone will be wearing them, Mom." *Translation: I want to look better than all my friends.* Dad was surprised, though. Told me to return them when he'd seen the credit card bill. Too late, I'd said. Already worn them. *Translation: No freaking way.* But that was before. When I still believed that she who collects the most envious stares is happiest. I miss those days. Being shallow. It's like living in a pink mist of self-adoration. It's easy. Although now that the mist has cleared, I realize it was just an excuse for being a bitch. There's a perk to being in pain that I forgot to mention. It forces you to be nicer. To realize you aren't all that, after all. And, isn't the first step to fixing yourself simply recognizing your faults? I think I read that on the back of one of my mom's 12-steps to self-actualization books. I'm a long way off from working toward world peace, but at least I'm no longer laughing at girls with bad hair and ugly clothes. That's good, right? Sadly, they're laughing at me now. Mercy.

I draw a circle with my left toe around the wad of pink gum flattened against the speckled linoleum. Little good these boots did me now. Killer boots can't save a tattered reputation. I should write that on Facebook. Has a nice ring to it. But the new me doesn't post anymore. It tends to set off a string of scathing comments.

Suck it, bitch.
When will you shrivel up and die, already?
Slut. Slut. Slut. Slut. Slut.

I've come to the conclusion that people are assholes.

A couple of grade nines are talking by an open locker as I head down the hallway and out the door. They're the nerdy kind. With too-tight-in-the-ass grey pants and collars that stick out like bat wings to the tips of their shoulders. Harmless, though. Not even a hushed glance as I walk by. I have a sliver of hope that maybe not every student at Sacred Heart has seen the photo. At least not the ones that are too immersed in video games to waste time looking at boobs.

I park on the street in front of my house, cringing when I hear the scrape of tree branches against the roof. Dad's home from work early, and his car is parked on the driveway. A yellow Volkswagen Beetle is beside it. One of those really old ones, like from nineteen-sixty-five, or something. The license plate reads AutoMedic. *Sweet.*

Dude must be here to give a quote on fixing my Civic. I turn back to look at the dents on the hood. More on the passenger's side. I feel the anger rising the longer I stare at it. *Found it this way when I came out of the mall last week. Horrible, isn't it? Who would do such a thing?* At least that was the story I told Dad. He couldn't argue. After all, I'd parked in the outskirts, just like he'd taught me to do in public lots. Less chance of getting dinged, he'd say. He knew as well as I did, though, that the story didn't make sense. Who's going to take a bat, or golf club, or whatever, to a car in a shopping centre parking lot in the early evening? Certainly not a stranger.

"Do you think this was done by people who know you?" He'd asked in a steady voice. Careful not to alarm me to the possibility that there may exist a group of people who aren't fond of me.

"I dunno." A shrug, an eyebrow lift, and shifting of the eyes. A stone-cold lie.

The front door opens as I'm about to walk in. Dad is shaking hands with a round faced woman with equally round sunglasses. Short curly brown hair, the faint outline of a moustache that shouldn't be there, and a gentle sneer that almost disappears when she says hello to me. Total butch. That's what the old me would have labelled her. But the new me, well, the new Lana is working hard to not judge others by their appearances. The same way I'm trying to not swear so much. We'll get to the world peace thing eventually. Baby steps.

"I'll take good care of her for you," the butch who shouldn't be called a butch says to me with a curt nod of her head.

"Awesome!" I can't wait to see it gleaming like a lollypop. "When will I get it back?"

"Hmm?" She tips her head. The sneer is back with harsh lines bending around her small tight mouth.

"We'll see you tomorrow morning," Dad interrupts, holding his arm out to direct the woman to her car. "Nice to meet you." He flicks his thumb at me, motioning toward the front door. "Go on inside, Lana. We'll talk in a minute."

"What the fu- fudge is there to talk about?" I mutter, walking into the hallway and tossing my bag to the floor. Something in the way he stiffened when he saw me has me feeling paranoid. Mom's in the kitchen pouring red wine into a blue-coloured drinking glass.

"Lana!" She lifts the wine bottle and freezes like she's being busted for shoplifting. "You're home already?"

I open the fridge and pull out a Diet Coke. "It's three. I'm always home now." Leaning against the counter I stare at her. She sets the bottle on the counter and pushes it into the corner beside the flour and sugar canisters. Like now I won't notice that she's already into the booze.

"How was your day?" She asks, running her fingers through her blonde hair with one hand while the other strums against the counter.

"Awesome. What's going on with my car?"

Bringing the glass to her mouth, she sips her wine, then looks out the window. Pretends she doesn't hear me.

"Leaves are starting to change colour." I know better than to repeat myself. When Mom avoids my questions, something is up. She is the purveyor of good news only. *We're going on a cruise! I've made your favourite dinner! You're getting a car!*

That's how I know they're not fixing my car before Dad even tells me. She can't pretty this story up. Dad's the bad news guy. Or, in many cases, he's simply the reality check. When Mom says we've booked a cruise for the family, Dad explains it's on a river boat down the St. Lawrence with Grandma and Granddad in tow. Even his good news is interpreted as bad. When I'm not pissed off at him, I feel sorry for him.

I'm stuffing a chocolate chip cookie in my mouth when Dad walks in and stands with his arm around Mom's shoulders. His lips are tightly drawn, nostrils flared.

"We have to talk to you about something, Lana." He turns to Mom for support. But she's still gazing out the window at the damn leaves.

"I know. You're not fixing my car," I say, grabbing another cookie. "So, how long am I stuck driving around in that pockmarked thing? It's a bit embarrassing, to be honest." Mostly because I know the people who did it giggle and point every time I pull into the school parking lot.

"Ah," big exhale. "Lana, uh, you won't be driving it anymore." He drops his arm from Mom's shoulders. He knows as well as I do that any effort to look like a united couple is a sham. "We're selling it. Tomorrow it's getting picked up."

My mouth drops. Do I hear this right? *Prison.* The word echoes through my head. My car was my one guaranteed escape from everyone at school. How many times in the past two weeks had I slipped out of school early, hopped into my car and driven to the mall, the coffee shop, the anywhere-but-here. *But you're taking away my freedom!* I wish I could say it. Tell them how hellish my life has become. Show them the texts. The Facebook comments. Give them a glimpse.

"It's too expensive to repair, Lana." Dad explains. "When we bought the car..." He looks down at the counter and presses his fingertips together. "A lot has changed since then. With my job. Our income. Frankly, we don't have the money."

The clang of prison doors. Forcing my tongue to push the cookie down my throat, I allow myself to speak. Don't scream. Just talk in a normal tone.

"How will I get to and from school every day?" I'm trying too hard to stay calm. The words come out jagged and forced. Mom stares at me now. Her jaw tense and square. She's fearful that this will erupt into a pre-menstrual-esque explosion of emotions. And by emotions, I mostly mean self-pity. It's been my modus operandi for years and I'm not particularly proud of it, but like my propensity to swear like a drunken truck driver and make fun of ugly or weird people, this one is a hard habit to break. But look at me now. I'm making progress. Before I turned into the most hated person in my school, I would have never had the insight to recognize these faults in myself. I love it when I can find an upside to my crap life.

"You'll be taking the bus." Dad's words come at me like daggers. I actually fall back and clutch my chest.

"I'm in grade twelve, Dad!" I half-cough, half spit. "Only losers take the bus at my age. Are you kidding me?"

Dad folds his arms and shakes his head. "I am sorry that things are not working out the way you'd hoped but we are all making sacrifices. You start tomorrow morning. I'm sure your friends will still like you."

"That's not really my biggest concern," I mutter, swallowing my anger. If I let a word slip about my friends then it could snowball into a full confession. And we can't have that. Now, not only am I the biggest slut in school, I'll be the biggest loser. This might all be manageable if I was on a reality show. They could call it *High School Girls*. I'd be the girl that everyone roots for because don't all viewers love the underdog? Hundreds of tweets packed with short-form words of support. Thousands of Facebook friends commenting on how far I've fallen. From popular girl to bus-riding loner. She's suffered enough, they'd claim. If a camera were on me now, I'd cue the tears. Get the fans riled up. Instead, I storm upstairs to my room, slamming the door behind me. Another bad habit. God, I have a lot to work on.

Pulling my phone from my pocket, I stare at the screen saver of me and Alysa blowing kisses at the camera. Can't believe I haven't changed it yet. After everything she's put me through. I try to throw the phone across the room but it rebounds off the corner of my bed and lands back at my feet. Sliding down the wall and onto the carpet, I stretch my legs out and pick the phone back up. Rub the fingerprints off the screen and scroll through my photos until I settle on a selfie that, not too long ago, earned over two hundred Facebook likes. I look pretty, thanks to the lash extensions I had done that day. It's better than my fake friend screen saver. I replace it and hit *Save*.

Reading my messages, I see the last one I received was from Mom this morning telling me to have a great day (sideways smiley face!) Another reminder of my loser life.

I scroll down to Stu's messages. I sent him five this morning. All variations of 'Where the hell are you?' He has yet to respond. I know it's probably because he leaves his phone at home most days. Our school has a firm no mobile phone policy that most students ignore. Stu excepted. I've often wondered if he purposely leaves it elsewhere so that I can, also, remain elsewhere. Another hint that it's time to dump him. I need another reason like I need a nail in my brain. It's thanks to him that the photo went viral. I hate him almost as much as I hate the fabbies. *Almost.* But he's my last connection to them, and by them, I mean the source of all that defines popular, beautiful, and worthy at Sacred Heart. Stu represents the single thread from which all my hope hangs that one day, soon, I'll be back in the game. They say there's a fine line between love and hatred, so I figure it wouldn't be so hard to flip from the dark side, if given the chance. I type him a message.

What r u doing? My day has gone from bad to worse

Then I delete it before hitting send. Leave the phone on the floor as I crawl to my bed and climb under its covers. I know he'll text me later when he's ready for some action. He's dependable, that way. It lessens the loneliness in the smallest way.

Chapter 2

Library Refugee

The bus is heavy with warm air and body odour. All eyes are on me as I stand awkwardly in the middle aisle, running my fingers through my damp hair. I wish I'd looked outside before leaving the house this morning. Then I'd have known to bring an umbrella. My shoes squeak against the rubber matting. Scanning for an empty seat, I try to avoid eye contact with the zombified faces pointed in my direction. I know they're staring, not out of any particular interest, but from a simple lack of distractions. *Find a seat. Find a freaking seat.* They're all taken save a couple half-empty ones. With a deep breath, I twirl and drop into the first free spot to my left, hugging my bag against my chest. The green leather seat in front of me has the words 'School sux' scrawled in black capital letters.

"Nice day, huh?" The guy beside me says.

"The worst," I answer without glancing at him.

"You're in grade twelve, right?" He asks. I nod and turn to face him. He looks about my age, but I don't recognize him. A dark blue toque is pulled over his head with dark cowlicks curling out from under it. His face is thin and milky white except for the flush of pink on his cheeks. He smiles crookedly at me. I force my mouth to return the smile, but my stomach is twisting as I prepare myself for some kind of snide comment about the photo.

"Yeah," I say cautiously. "You?"

"Yep," he answers. When the bus suddenly jerks to a stop, we both instinctively grip the seat in front of us to soften the whiplash.

The bus starts rolling again and I look at him more closely. "Are we in any classes together?" He's actually pretty cute, in a tortured-artist kind of way.

"No. I'm in the EC program," he says before looking back out his window.

"The enriched stream." I relax a bit. A science geek. Maybe he hasn't seen the photo. "You're new?"

"Yeah," he answers. "We moved here at the end of the summer. Welcome to the land of the lame."

I laugh. "We're lame? Aren't you too busy studying the Periodic table to party?"

"I wasn't talking about partying." He points his gaze at me for so long I start to squirm. "That's the problem with this place. All anyone cares about is how many beers you can guzzle. Pathetic, really."

I straighten my back against the seat and turn away. I hate this school more than anyone, but still his words offend me. Talking like he's better than us. Even if it is true, he's being an idiot.

13

"You sure you're not just jealous?" I ask. It's a weird knee-jerk reaction and I want to kick my own butt for saying it. I run my hands over my damp hair and twist it into a ponytail before letting go. *Why am I defending these people?*

"No, I'm not jealous. Just stating my thoughts, that's all," he says, nudging his toque higher up his forehead. "Maybe I just don't get this place. Well, that's not right. I definitely don't get this place. But that doesn't matter much. I just have to stick it out for a year. Ten months and I'm out."

I smile. So, I'm not the only one counting down the months, the days, sometimes the minutes until I can leave this school for good.

"I hear ya," I nod, catching his eye. He laughs. It's a quiet chuckle, but his eyes crinkle softly at the corners and I find myself disappointed by how quickly his face turns serious again.

"Pretty sad, isn't it? To live so many days just waiting for them to be finished? Seems such a waste." He sighs and looks ahead. Shrugs.

"I guess," I add. "But you've got to get through the day one way or the other. Use whatever works, right?" I press my lips together. I'm saying too much. He doesn't need to know I'm miserable. Next thing I know, he'll be asking why I have no friends. Why I can't wait to graduate. And why aren't I having the time of my life this last year of high school? I tighten my bag against my chest.

"Why are you so eager to graduate?" he asks. Right on cue. My stomach grinds.

"Oh, I'm not. Just hate the school work, you know?" I force a laugh that has me sounding more like a donkey than the sexy thing that I like to think I'm capable of being.

14

I clamp my mouth shut. This is an awkward moment I could have lived without. Thank goodness the bus is rolling into the school parking lot. I open my bag pretending to look for something, then zip it shut just as the bus doors slide open. *Mercy.* Jumping from the seat, I try to race ahead of him, but instead find myself waiting for the three rows ahead to file off first.

"See you later?" he asks, standing next to me. His arm brushing mine. With a quick nod, I raise my eyebrows and mutter something that sounds sort of like yes. When I step off the bus, I rush ahead. Don't turn around to say good-bye.

Mr. Zinsky, the school principal, is holding the front door open as I step through it. "Good morning Miss Tiller," he says in an annoyingly triumphant tone.

"Morning Mr. Zinsky," I mumble with a brief lift of my eyes. His black unibrow dips as he lets the door close behind us and shakes his finger at me.

"I hear you're taking your studies more seriously."

I nod, my eyes focused on his blue and red striped tie. "I guess."

"Good for you. All that time in the library will pay off. You keep up that attitude. There is no substitute for hard work." He's known for his motivational one-liners. And, by motivating, I mean annoying. Rumour has it he keeps a book of quotes in his office, memorizing a different one every day to try out on his flock.

"Okay," I say, but I'm not sure he hears me because he's already barking at someone for throwing a basketball in the hallway. I assume he's referring to my new survival technique. Sitting by myself in a library cubicle during the lunch hours that I don't take off in my car. It's just easier some days to stay at school, eat my sandwich and count down the minutes until the bell rings. Of course it's no surprise that he thinks I'm doing homework the entire time, but I can't seem to focus long enough to get much done. I've taken to reading the thesaurus when I'm super bored. Picking out words that I'd never think to use on my own. Like calumniator. Someone who makes malicious statements about another. I found it in the list of synonyms for 'bitch.' Zinsky is bound to be more impressed soon, now that my escape vehicle is gone for good.

I turn the hallway corner and see Stu's broad back leaning against my locker. This is a surprise considering I bailed on him last night. Call me a prude, but it's hard to get into a pleasing mood when your boyfriend sends a text that reads *Im horny. Want to com over?* At least I was kind enough to delete my first response – *Want to kiss my ass?* But even after my gently phrased *Not tonite*, the stench of girlfriend guilt stuck to me for hours. Keep Stu happy or risk losing him to the next girl in line. That's how it works with a guy like him. And by that, I mean hot guys. It's a daily struggle to adhere to it when his capacity to be a jerk grows ever apparent. I'm exhausted just thinking about it.

I force a smile on my face as I move toward him, ready to wrap my arms around his waist and act all pretty when I realize he's not waiting for me. I watch Melanie sidle up to him and grab his wrist. She stands on her tiptoes to whisper something in his ear. He laughs. I can't remember the last time I made him laugh. Even longer since he made me laugh.

"Move, please," I mutter, pushing my hand behind him to reach my lock and lightly shove him away.

He steps away from my locker and looks at me, his face contorted into a sneer. "Someone got up on the wrong side of the bed this morning."

"Shut up," I mutter. So much for my plans to please him.

"You shut up," he responds. We sound like my parents.

"Hi Lana," Melanie interrupts. Boyfriend thief. I have to watch out for these younger girls. They'll do anything for a senior. I should know.

"Hey," I say, finally turning to look at them both.

Stu laughs, his knuckles folded against his mouth. "Holy crap! What's with your face?"

"What's with yours?" I stupidly retort. Whipping the locker open, I glance at my reflection in the mirror on the inside of the door. Black mascara has smudged below my eyes, presumably from waiting for the bus in the rain. I think back to the cute guy on the bus and cringe with embarrassment. I wonder why he didn't say anything. Is that a nice guy thing? I wouldn't know.

"Want this?" Melanie hands me a tissue. I grab it and wet it with my tongue before dabbing my face.

"Thanks," I muster, stealing a glance at her. Her wheat coloured hair shimmers in thick waves past her shoulders. No black roots. Probably just got her highlights done. Or worse, it's natural. I shouldn't hate her. Melanie is one of the only girls who has not succumbed to hurling insults and backpacks at me. I don't get it. Why doesn't she hate me like everyone else?

"Melanie's trying out for the lead in the school musical. She's nervous," Stu says. Just the thing I want to hear. Not only does she look and act like an angel, she sings like one, too.

"Good luck." I say woodenly.

"Thanks," Melanie nods her head and waves, her long fingers tickling the air. "Talk to you later." Stu stares at her walk down the hallway. My face now clean, I rummage

17

through my locker for a spare cardigan to replace the soaked one, and grab my math books. The bell rings.

"She's too sweet for you." I hear a knife edge in my voice.

"Huh? What are you talking about?" Stu looks at me. I bite my lower lip. He's all I've got left here. The only person who still talks to me. The last thread tying me to the fabbies. I take in his light blue eyes, full lips, and dark brown hair cascading perfectly across his forehead. And, God, he's just so beautiful to look at.

"Nothing," I answer quickly.

"Later," Stu winks. "I have a free half hour after school. Your place or mine?"

"Can you drive me home?" I ask, ignoring his question. I'll do anything to avoid taking that awful bus again. I guess, even *that*. If I have the energy. I know I don't have the desire. Not these days, anyways.

"What's wrong with your car?"

"It's gone." I don't feel like talking about it, which is fine with Stu. He stares at me with his usual nonchalance. Like he's picking out toppings for a burger. Even still, he's stunningly good looking. A face worth admiring no matter how dense it appears. That's why I worked so hard to get my claws into him this summer. Learning his work schedule to coincidentally appear at the end of his shifts. Laughing at all his dumb jokes. Dropping hints at what I'd do for him if he gave me the chance. Exhausting, yes. But effective. Unfortunately, he came complete with a steady line of girls ready to carry the girlfriend torch the second I stumble out of favour. It's nothing short of tragic that the excitement that once fluttered like a butterfly in my stomach whenever I saw him is now dead. Suffocated the night he took the photo. Still, I hang on.

"So, your place," he says as one of his football buddies punches him in the arm. Twirling toward him, he attempts to return the favour, but misses.

"So, you're driving me home," I say to his back as he disappears down the hallway chasing his friend, knocking down a skinny student in a red baseball cap along the way. I'm going to assume that's a yes for both of us.

***

I miss looking forward to things. Those quiet boosts of anticipation that drive you through the shitty parts of life. I used to get them so often that I never noticed them until they were gone. Now, my emotions flip between dread and indifference. One miserable experience rolls after the other. Like lunch period. A perfect example of something I used to look forward to.

Standing outside the cafeteria, I lean my back against the wall in a lame attempt to go unnoticed. A group of students walks by me, slowing to open the doors. I count eight feet. Four girls. Their voices drop to a hush. I feel my cheeks warm.

"She's that girl," says one, loud enough for me to hear.

"The one in the photo?" This one is a bit quieter. Thanks for that.

"Gross!" Two in unison.

Legs finally shuffle past the door into the lunchroom. I stare through the gap between the door and the wall, looking beyond the girls to see throngs of students seated around the tables, chatting and eating like they haven't a care in the world. Is it worth the risk for some food? I wipe the perspiration from my forehead. Lift my arms to let some air into my pits where I feel it growing sticky with wetness. I picture my lunch bag sitting on the kitchen counter where I'd left it. My stomach growls. I haven't stepped foot into the cafeteria in almost two weeks. Swallowing the knot rising toward my throat, I turn away. I'd rather starve, I decide, than walk through that crowd. Head down, I beeline it to the library and ram into someone's chest.

"Whoa!" Arms wrap around my shoulders, pulling me close. I look up and groan. Fitz.

"Sorry," I mutter, trying to shake his hands off of me. He hangs on to both my arms and looks me up and down.

"Hey Lana. What's the hurry? Got another photo shoot?" He laughs, jabbing his buddy next to him.

"Go to hell, Fitz," I hiss. I try to avoid him almost as much as his girlfriend, my ex-BFF, Alysa. Talk about the couple from hell. Predators, the both of them, set to the task of annihilating the self-worth of anyone who hovers near.

"I don't remember you posing for me when we went out," Fitz says, letting go of me so that I can rush past him.

I groan for lack of a better response. My gag reflex is activated every time I'm reminded of our short, yet highly regrettable, stint as sort-of-boyfriend-and-girlfriend. It was only a few dates, most of which involved going to parties together. And, to be perfectly honest, my only reason for putting up with him as long as I did was to make Stu jealous. A brilliant strategy that worked exactly as I'd hoped. The constant reminder of it is a downside I have yet to overcome.

His laugh echoes down the hallway as I rush toward the library, and step into the quiet room. A few heads turn my way. The regulars nod at me and I smile weakly. I've always assumed everyone else was here because of their steely dedication to academics, but when I notice a bruised eye on the Asian guy who always sits at the second table to the left, I think twice. Perhaps I'm not the only using this place as a refuge. *Library Loners.* There's an idea for a reality show. Revealing the secret lives of library kids one loser at a time.

On the way to my usual cubby, I glide by the shelf that holds the thesaurus. Grab it and lug it up to the second floor and thumb through the P's. *Psychopath.* What a disappointing selection. *Maniac. Nutcase.* None of them worthy of Fitz. Running my finger through the list, I finally settle on one. *Demoniac.*

I write it on the inside back cover of my English binder beneath calumniator. This probably wasn't what Ms. Laccetta had in mind when she wrote on my report *Expand your vocabulary!* It's a start, anyway.

I rub my arms vigorously with opposite hands, trying to remove any lingering Fitz touch from my body. There was something in the way he looked at me. I don't want to admit it scared me because that would make me paranoid. But something made me feel very uncomfortable. Even nervous. Deep down, a voice is warning me to stay away from him.

Chapter 3

Pride is Overrated

I'm tearing through the hallway to catch the bus, vaguely aware of the students shifting out of my way, thinking this is not how a person blends into the background. But I'd waited for Stu to show up at my locker, just like we'd agreed. Okay, I'm stretching the definition of agreed. We mutually, silently, sort of made a deal that he would drive me home in return for certain favours. I waited seven minutes. Too long. My only other ride will be rolling out of the school lot any second now.

Turning the corner, I can see past the doors where the buses are still lined up. I'll make it, I think, when I feel my right ankle hit something and lift into the air. I stumble to my knees and smack my hands against the floor to prevent my face from smashing against it.

"Loser."

I bristle at Alysa's voice. Sitting back on my calves, I turn to look darkly at her. She narrows her eyes at me and shakes her head, gathering her long black hair at the nape of her neck and flipping it over one shoulder. Petting it like a ferret.

"Why don't you crawl back into the hole you came from?" She says, then looks at Sarah standing to her right, and smirks. They're matching in black yoga pants, white hoodies, and purple hairbands. I have the same outfit at home. Today is Yoga Thursday. Every week at four o-clock they go straight to hot yoga. I'd been the one to organize it the first week of school. It was supposed to be for the three of us. My gut turns as they roll their eyes and walk around me. I hear the buses drive out of the parking lot.

I know I should stand up for myself. I've heard all the sound bites. The anti-bully slogans. *Be Happy – Bullies Hate It! Bullying is for Losers.* All lies. I'm the loser. Seriously. Look at me. A senior kneeling in the middle of the school hallway fighting back tears because I missed my bus. Someone hand me a sucker and ask, 'Where's your mommy?' and it'll be complete.

"Are you okay?" I glance up to see the toque guy from this morning extending his hand. I groan. What little pride may have remained in reserve is officially depleted.

"Yeah. Thanks," I mutter as he helps lift to me to my feet. We walk side by side. When he holds the door open I notice a tattoo on his left arm. A line of script that snakes around his forearm. I shift my eyes to his face. He's looking intently at me, like he's known me a lot longer than since this morning. It catches me off guard and I bang into the side of the door. *Mercy.*

"You missed the bus, too?" He asks.

23

"No. I have a drive home." The lie rolls off my tongue effortlessly.

"Lucky you." We stop at the end of the walkway. This is where I would wait if someone were to actually pick me up, so I drop my bag and look into the distance as if my drive will arrive any second.

"I had the worst day," he starts, then looks sideways at me. "Well, maybe not the worst." An awkward pause cues me to say something. Anything to alleviate the humiliating incident he'd witnessed minutes ago. I sigh.

"That honour probably goes to me today." I look at my watch, wondering how long I have to pretend I'm waiting to be picked up. "You said you just moved here. Where were you before?"

"Brooklyn," he replies.

"Really?" I stare at him, suddenly viewing him through a shiny lens of admiration. "Why would you leave New York City? No wonder you hate it here, living in this little pocket of dullsville."

"My mom grew up in Toronto and wanted to come back to be closer to her family."

"But Harristown is still a trek from Toronto. Not that Toronto is anything like New York City, but still, it's better than here."

He shrugs and kicks the toe of his shoe against the concrete. "A lot of shit happened last year. She needed a change. Brooklyn just wasn't cutting it, anymore. But, me? I just want to finish high school and get out of here. How about you? What's your story?"

"I don't have a story. Born and raised here, the land of the lame."

"So, girls just mess up other girls for the fun of it around here?"

"Something like that. I guess."

"I saw that girl trip you. The mean one with the long black hair. Saw her take you down, then walk by. You didn't say a word. Just sat there." His brow wrinkles. *You were pathetic.* I'm sure that's what he is thinking.

"Yeah, I know." I twirl a strand of hair. This conversation is officially uncomfortable. "She's my best friend, actually. But we're not really getting along right now."

"That's your best friend?" he asks, incredulous. "I think you need new friends." I breathe through my nostrils and slowly exhale. *It's slim pickings for me these days.*

"Don't you have to get home? Study the law of physics or something?" The words come out meaner than I'd planned. I watch a squirrel run circles around a tree, then race up its trunk.

"Ah, sorry," he throws his bag over his back. "I didn't mean to... what I mean is, if you feel like hanging out or something. I'm Demit, by the way. Not that you asked, but I'm in the book as the old folks used to say. The other book, now." Silence hangs between us for a few seconds.

I cock my head. "In the book?" I ask.

"Phone book? Facebook? I mean... Forget it." He shrugs as I stare at him. He's a nice guy. I could use a bit of that in my life right now.

"I don't go on Facebook anymore," I finally say. "But I'll see you around at school. My name is Lana."

"Nice to meet you." Demit lifts two fingers to his forehead, then taps a salute and turns. I watch his back as he travels down the street and disappears around a corner. Wait another few minutes before I start my own trek home so that he has a strong enough lead. I don't get very far before a silver minivan slows and stops beside me.

"Hey Lana," Stu says through his open window.

"You're late." *Translation: Asshole.*

"I had something. Don't go all bitchy on me." His thick brown hair is swept to one side. Lifting an eyebrow, he throws a dimpled grin my way. My mind registers his ridiculously handsome face but my heart is unmoved. I walk around the front of the minivan and open the passenger door to climb in.

"What about football?" I ask, buckling myself into the seat.

"Yeah, we don't have much time," he explains, shifting the gear into drive. "There's a park up here. We'll just have to use the backseat."

"I'd rather go home."

"Babe, I don't have time. The van is fine." I roll my eyes at his stupidity. I'd rather go home and crawl into bed. By. My. Self.

I'm quiet as he pulls into the park driveway and finds a spot under a huge oak. A mother is pushing a carriage past our van. I sink deep into my seat. Stu has already slipped to the back seat.

"What are you waiting for?" His voice is laced with urgency. Taking a deep breath, I climb between the two front seats to join him. There are so many things I'd rather be doing. Watching paint dry. Scrubbing pots. Unclogging a toilet. My hand lands on a sheet of paper, which I pick up to flick to the floor. A quick glance at it and my heart stops. A music sheet. The name 'Melanie' is written in red ink in the top right corner.

"You trying out for the school musical?" I ask, my voice a shard of glass. Stu tries to grab the paper. I pull away too soon and he misses. Scrunching it into a ball, I throw it in his face.

"Is that why you were late getting me? Trying to score with the hottie in grade eleven?" Lunging at him, I scratch the side of his face before he takes hold of my wrists and pins me against the seat. *Demoniac.* I'm the definition of demoniac right now. Bulging eyes. Smoke coming out of the ears. Guttural noises.

"After all I've done for you, this is how you treat me?" The words slither out and I want to strangle him with them. "Did you take a picture of her, too? Turn her into the next school slut? Let me guess, you're too nice to do that to her! Only I get that special treatment."

"Relax, Lana."

The rage that I'd compacted neatly inside my rib cage over the past two weeks explodes. Relaxation is not an option. "Don't tell me to relax!" I shriek. Stu releases my arm to reach past me and slide open the door. I grab his hair and pull as he shoves me off the seat and out of the car.

"Psycho!" He uncurls my fist from his hair then pushes me so hard I stumble to the concrete, scraping my knees. The door closes and the van peels away.

"It's over!" I yell over the squeal of tires. The van stops. Stu opens the door. *An apology?* My backpack is tossed to the ground. Then he's gone. And I'm left with a handful of brown hair and a long walk home.

***

They say walks are good for you. It turns out they're right, whomever they are. It takes me forty-five minutes to get home. Just my luck that Stu picks a park in the opposite direction of my house. Inconsiderate jerk. I've called him every curse word I could think of, exhausting my supply and resorting to making up new ones. That took up the first half of my autumn stroll. But it's hard to stay angry.

I wonder if there's a natural limit to how long we can be door-slamming, curse-screaming mad. For me? Seems to be about twenty minutes. It was around that time when I reminded myself of the new Lana rules. Be nice. Don't judge. Don't swear. (Not sure I'll ever master that last one.) Which is why Stu is an inconsiderate jerk, instead of that long, curse-laden name I made up at the start of the walk.

By the time I turn onto my street, I'm even thinking that I may have overreacted to the music sheet. If I hadn't tried to scratch his eyeballs out, he might have had an opportunity to explain why it was there. It is possible that he has a perfectly good explanation. Although it's a desperate thought. One of many I've had over the past two weeks. And then there's the whole issue of me telling him it's over. I'm troubled by that. Not sure that I'm ready to let go of my final fabbie connection. Once he's gone, it'll be official. I'm a nobody.

Chapter 4

A Glimmer of Hope

The room is dark. I napped longer than I'd planned. A door slams downstairs and heavy shoes step across the hardwood floor. Dad is just getting home, which means it should be dinner soon. Without flicking on the light, I peel off my uniform and slip into pyjamas. I debate whether I want to venture downstairs or climb back under my covers. Opening my door a crack, I listen to their conversation.

"Where's Lana," Dad says. Clattering of dishes as he pulls out plates and cutlery for dinner.

"In her room. Where do you think?" Mom sounds irritable. "You took away her car. Do you think she wants to even see us?"

Fighting words. I grimace. So, the car was all Dad's idea. Just as I suspected. I open the door a bit more and tiptoe to the top of the stairs.

"Did you tell her that?" His voice is gritty. "That this is all me? For Christ's sake, Cynthia. You need to grow up, too. One kid is enough in the house."

"How da-a-are you!" The way she draws out the word dare, I suspect she's had a few. Helps explain why she was asleep on the sofa when I got home. Silence. More clatter. Microwave door opening and closing. Beeps. Hum.

"I don't want to fight," Dad's voice is low. I strain to hear it. "Please, Cynthia. Put that away." She's having a drink. Microwave door opens and shuts.

"Don't tell me what to do, Kevin." Her voice is shrill.

"So you've spoken to Lana?" Dad uses his patient voice. Like he's speaking to an eight-year-old. "Of course she's going to be upset. I understand that. But it's not just about teaching her to be more responsible. Which we are failing miserably at. It's also about money. We can't afford the car. We're broke, for God's sake. We spend more than I earn. Well, let's be honest here. You spend more than I earn. The money tree has dried up. And fixing a beaten-up car that we couldn't afford in the first place is just plain dumb."

"Don't start blaming me for everything."

"I'm not... Forget it. I can't talk to you when you're like this. Did you just open this bottle today? It's empty."

"Don't you try changing the subject."

I don't want to hear anymore. Slipping back into my room, I quietly close the door. We're broke. This would have crippled the old me who had a mental list of must-have items to slowly check off through the Fall. Coach purse, yoga pants, sparkly slip-on shoes, jeans, two bracelet charms. None of them matter now. My uniform, rumpled on the floor, is all I need these days. And comfy pyjamas.

I flip open my laptop. Click on Facebook. Stupid idea, of course. I'd last visited the site five days ago. There were fifty-seven notifications, kindly alerting me to a list of 'we-hate-Lana' comments and threats. That was partly my fault, though. I get it now. Lesson learned. Never try to defend yourself online. You can't win.

I'm going online for one purpose only today. Delete my profile. My friend count has been dwindling. Seventy-three unfriended. The other seven hundred and three friends don't know me beyond my selfies and 'Aren't I amazing?' posts. Not that it stops them from taking a ride on the Lana-sucks-ass train. That's the other lesson I learned. Don't accept every friend request, especially those with photos of men in their thirties. Turns out they're creepy.

A friend request is waiting. I haven't had one of those in a while. Demit Solokov. A pocket of sweetness unwraps somewhere deep in my chest. *I have a new friend.* I click accept before remembering why I'd come online in the first place. Burying my embarrassment at being so smitten by a single friend request, I wallow in the pleasure of knowing somebody out there likes me. Then the reality of what I've done smacks me squarely on the forehead. I've just given Demit full access to my posts. Not. Good. Recommitting to my Facebook suicide, I click on settings when his name pops up on chat. He's such a welcome change from the solitude, I respond immediately.

DEMIT: Hey Lana. Did ur ride come?
LANA: Yep.
DEMIT: Lucky u. Took me forever to walk home.
LANA: Its a long walk. Hate that.
DEMIT: U taking bus tomorrow?
LANA: O ya.
DEMIT: I'll save u a seat.

LANA: Bus sucks. Almost as much as walking but what can u do?
DEMIT: Ya. I saw some of the mean girls on my way home. Drove by me. One of them gave me the finger. WTF? Haters gotta hate.
LANA: Sounds like them, all right.
DEMIT: I know you call them friends, but that's messed up. IMHO.

My mom opens the door. "Lana?" She peeks into my room. "Hmm."

"Can I turn on the light?" She doesn't wait for a reply and the lights flick on. I quickly type my last message to Demit.

PIR. CWYL.

I type my cell number and shut the laptop before Mom gets too close.

"I know how upsetting it must be to lose your car."

"Uh-huh."

"So, I got you something." A plastic bag rustles. "To sort of make up for it. I know it's not your car, but..."

I'm silent. Dad just finished telling her that we're broke and this is where she takes it? Beaming, she drops the bag on my bed, waiting for me to reciprocate her big fake smile.

"I don't want it."

"You don't even know what it is." Pulling the bag handles apart, she lifts the purse I'd begged her to buy all summer. Dropping it on top of my laptop, she waits, holding her breath.

I can't remember why I wanted this. It's a hideous pink with a gold buckle across the middle.

"I don't need it. But, thanks."

Mom grabs it and frames it between her hands like she's on The Shopping Channel.

32

"All your friends will be jealous." Wide-eyed, she looks at me, almost nervously, like I'm forgetting my line. Her shoulders hunched in expectation.

"Return it, Mom. We don't have the money."

"Of course we do. It's just a little bag." She drops it on my bed and runs her fingers through her short blonde hair, then smiles stiffly. "But, whatever you want."

It's hard to get Mom to act angry. It's not in her repertoire because, believe me, she's always acting. Wearing the smile. Making up for the acting career she never had. She'd moved to California before I was born to pursue her dream. The way she tells it, she scored a gig in a toothpaste commercial within two weeks of arriving in Hollywood. "Make your smile shine." It was the first line she'd ever said in front of a camera, and everyone back home had been giddy with small town pride that she'd be the next big thing. Still says it every time someone takes a snapshot. Christmas dinners. Graduations. Amusement parks. Cocks her head to the side and smiles like she's got the whitest teeth this side of the Atlantic. It had been both her debut and her pinnacle. Nothing followed.

I found the video on YouTube a little while back. Finally got to see what all the fuss was about. Her long blonde hair is flipped back. Little red shorts, white tank top, and tanned shoulders. She walks toward a tall hunk of a man, sets her hands on his shoulders, and turns to flash her dazzling ivories. "Make your smile shine." She looks beautiful. I've watched it hundreds of times, trying to pick out at least one feature that I share with her. We both have straight, white teeth. That's about it. Thank you, braces and Crest Whitestrips.

"Mom?"

"Yes, Lana?"

"Why did you leave California?" It seems an odd time to ask about this, but I feel this pressing need to know her better. Like, right now. Tell me a bit about you, I think. And I'll tell you a bit about me.

"You know why," Mom says. "I missed your dad too much. He wouldn't move south, so I came back." Her voice is wooden. She's either lying or sanitizing regret from her tone. "Then we got married."

"Really? You missed him that much, eh?"

She stifles a yawn and stares past me. "It's dinner time. Dad is waiting."

***

Midnight. I can't sleep. Pulling my phone out from under my pillow, I stare at the screen. Tap on messages. Tap on photos. Tap on Candy Crush. I should take up smoking. It would give my antsy fingers something to do. I wonder if Demit is awake. A clear act of desperation to be texting a guy I just met, but I like him. There, I admit it. I like the guy. So why should I feel weird about wanting to text him? I read the message he sent two hours ago.

Waddup?

I type in Hi and hit send, then stash the cell phone back under my pillow and try to forget about it, hoping it will force patience into my fidgety mind. My phone beeps. I'm so excited, I actually clap.

DEMIT: Hi Lana. Sup.
LANA: Cant sleep. U?
DEMIT: Doing homework still.

LANA: Yuck.
DEMIT: Why cant u sleep? Stressed out?
LANA: Yah. My life. Serious suck mode.
DEMIT: With friends like urs. Can't say I'm surprised.
What's going on?
LANA: Ah. the usual. Lost all my friends, have a total
asshole for a boyfriend and went from queen b to
desperate loser. No friends. No life. No fun. FML.
DEMIT: Don't FYL. Ur better off without them.
LANA: Thanks, but reality check. Im nobody without
them. Boyfriend is a jerk, but all I got.
DEMIT: He's holding u back. U gotta lose the extra
baggage.
LANA: Not that easy. I do hate him
DEMIT: Good. That's a clear sign you should leave him
LANA: Be easier if he just disappeared. All of them
disappear. Just fall off the face of the planet.
DEMIT: Or die.
LANA: Hmm. Ya that would work. Of natural causes,
of course!
DEMIT: It was a joke...
LANA: LOL. I know.
DEMIT: Gotta get back to physics
LANA: K
DEMIT: TTYL
LANA: K

Stuffing my phone under my pillow, I shut my eyes and
cross my forearms over my chest where I feel a rush of
warmth. But there's something else. Something new. I
think it's hope.

Chapter 5

Finish What You've Started

Leaning against the fence that surrounds the football field, I wonder for the thousandth time what possessed me to agree to meet Stu after his game. If Stu heard me break up with him yesterday as he peeled away in his minivan, he showed no sign of it today. We went through our usual routine. Stu standing by my locker when I arrive in the morning. Me getting ticked off the second he opens his mouth (what does he expect when he starts the conversation with 'Did you take your chill pill today.') Us sort-of making up before the bell rings and sort-of agreeing to meet after school, or in the case of today – after his game – which is why I'm standing here watching a boring football game rather than sitting on the school bus. At least the sun is shining and there's a nice warm breeze. Hard not to feel a little optimistic on days like this.

Leaning against the fence, I lift my head upward and close my eyes, letting the sun warm my skin. Let my mind wander into fantasy where my life is perfect. Stu apologizes for throwing me out of his van. He explains why Melanie's music was there and it makes perfect sense! Silly me. Then tells me he loves me. My eyes flutter open and I squint into the sun. God, I'm delusional. I need to break up with him for once and for all. He's a lying, sociopathic son-of-a-bitch. But do I have the nerve to leave him today? That's up for debate.

I have a whole hour of waiting around, wondering whether I should dump him or keep him. Dump him or keep him. If I keep him, I'd better be prepared to deliver the goods after yesterday's epic fail. I can barely stand to think about it. It doesn't help that I'm inundated with girls calling me a slut all day. One stupid photo and every girl thinks I'm sex-crazed for any guy that walks in a room. If anything, this whole situation has had the opposite effect.

I think about Demit's text last night. 'Or die.' I feel guilty that the word so accurately reflects my desire. Not that I really want the fabbies dead. Like real dead. Do I? Wouldn't that make me a monster? I silence the thought. It's not like I could ever, in any way, be responsible for anyone's death. Even if a small part of me would be happy if a couple of them died, it makes no difference in the world. Life without Alysa would be pretty darn awesome. I let that thought sit in my head. Nothing wrong with that.

My phone vibrates. It's a text from Demit.

DEMIT: What r u doing?
LANA: Don't ask.
DEMIT: U r ...fill-in-blank
LANA: At football game.
DEMIT: .... stunned silence... Because?

LANA: Meeting stu after
DEMIT: Ah. Stay away from mean girls
LANA: I will
DEMIT: Promise?
LANA: Oh ya. U don't need to convince me!

I stuff my phone inside my jacket and turn just in time to see Stu tackle a player to the ground. Everyone in the stands cheers. I clap for three seconds. After two years of attending school football games, I still don't understand what any of it means. More importantly, I still don't care.

Sticking buds into my ears, I scroll through my playlist when a sharp object hits my back. Turning, I find myself face to face with Alysa, Sarah, and Tracy huddling before me. A rock lays just past my foot. They've resorted to stoning. *Really?* I cross my arms over my chest and stare back at them.

"Why are you here?" Alysa asks. Sunlight glints off her shiny lips.

"Could you just leave me alone? I'm not bugging anyone."

"Stu is so over you," Tracy blows back, flipping her hand. She's changed out of her uniform and is in tight jeans and a cream sweater with a deep v-neck. She must be wearing a push-up to show so much cleavage. "He's told everyone that he's dumping you tonight, so why don't you just make it easy and disappear now. Nobody wants to see you here."

I surprise myself by laughing. "Oh, really? He's dumping me?" *A little late, Stu. I've already dumped you.*

"Yeah, and we can smell your slut wreak from a mile away. Go home and have a bath, would you?" Tracy adds with a smirk, flipping her blonde hair behind her shoulders.

I always hated Tracy. Ugly no matter how thick her fake eyelashes are or how big her boobs look. It's such a stupid insult, that I want to laugh at her. But, for some reason it hurts more than the other ones. I look at the ground. *I know I don't smell. Do I?*

"Let's go," Alysa says, leading them toward the stands and away from me. "Trust me. She'll leave."

I pick up the rock and consider aiming it at the back of Tracy's head, but I'm a terrible thrower. Instead, I turn back to watch the game, determined to stay put and prove that I can withstand whatever they throw at me, large sharp stones excepted.

I won't leave. I won't leave. I repeat it over and over, even as my feet turn from the fence and march toward the school. *Dammit. I'm leaving.*

Melanie is exiting the library as I'm about to walk in. She holds the door open for me so I can skirt by her.

"Hey," she mumbles.

"Hey." I step past her, then stop, take in a deep breath, and rush back out the doors. "Melanie?"

She freezes and turns her head so that I can only see her profile. "Yeah?"

"Were you in Stu's van yesterday?" This isn't the first time I've confronted a girl about her interest in my boyfriend, but the usual confidence in my voice is gone. My voice cracks, instead. I'm getting too used being silent. I've lost my edge.

She sighs, tilts her head back, and slowly turns around. "Why? What did he tell you?"

"He said nothing happened. But I don't believe him. I know you're into him. I get it. The hot senior, but trust me, you can't handle a guy like Stu." The words rush out desperately like I'm pleading for my life.

Her pink lips drop open. "I don't want him. Of course he told you nothing happened!"

"So something did happen. I knew it!"

"He drove me home, well, wait. That's stretching the truth. He offered to drive me home, then stopped the van and started climbing all over me. I tried to push him off but he wouldn't quit until I was yelling at him to stop."

"So, you guys didn't do anything?"

She closes her eyes. "Did you hear me? He attacked me. What do you think I'm going to say? When he finally stopped, you want to know what he did?"

I could guess. I watch her face turn pink and eyes blink rapidly like she's fighting back tears. "He kicked me out of the car. Just left me there to walk home!"

"Two for two," I mutter.

"What?"

"Nothing. Stu doesn't take the word no very well."

"Listen," she looks around as if a spy might be hiding in a corner recording our clandestine conversation for the next issue of Seventeen magazine. "Stu may be hot, but he's scum. I know everyone blames you for the photo, but I don't. Wasn't he the one to take the photo and send it out?"

I'm stunned to silence for a few seconds before I can squeak out a response. "Yeah," I say. "Pretty much." Melanie is the first person to understand the truth. It relieves some of the ache that's been pulling at my chest for the past two weeks.

"How can you want anything to do with him?" She shakes her head and sneers. "I've got to go. My mom will be waiting outside." She shrugs and disappears around the corner while I ponder what she said. I decide, right then, that I'm going to end it with Stu. As much as I feel like going home now, I know if I stick around until the end of the game I'm less likely to chicken out. Walking into the empty library, I flop into chair the closest to the door and wait.

***

I hang outside the locker room and watch guys file out one at a time, their hair soaked from sweat. Helmet and shoulder pads in one hand, bag in the other. Standing in a corner, I'm grateful that they don't notice me. At least ten guys have come out, but no sign of Stu. My stomach twists nervously. *Are you really ready to dump him? Be a nobody? Be alone?* That voice has spent the past forty minutes torturing my psyche. Doing its best to weaken my resolve. But I remain firm in my plan. Lose the excess baggage.

I wander closer to the door, expecting Stu will exit any minute. Instead, Fitz walks out. I jerk my head in the opposite direction, pretending not to see him.

"Lana." My skin crawls at the sound of his slippery voice. "What are you doing here?"

"I'm waiting for Stu." I answer coolly. "I said I'd meet him here after the game." Why am I explaining myself? I fold my arms over my chest.

"Stu?" He creeps up next to me and grabs my elbow. "You didn't watch the game, did you?"

I look at him from the corner of my eye. "No. I went to the library. Why?"

"Hmmm," he rubs his chin with his hand and stares intently at me. "He got injured. Why don't you just go in. Stu's the only one in there, now." Smooths his wavy brown hair with his hand, rests it on the back of his neck, and waits for my answer.

"No thanks. I'll wait."

"Just go! I'm serious. All the guys are gone. Surprise him. He'll love it. He's been talking about you." His eyebrows jump into his forehead as he gives me a jab in the ribs.

I don't believe him, but I decide it's easier to pretend I'm going in rather than be stuck listening to this jerk. "Yeah, sure. Okay." I step around Fitz and rest my hand on the door. I fake a step forward and wait for Fitz to take off down the hallway. But he doesn't budge. Just smiles at me.

A nervous laugh slips from my lips. "Okay, bye." I wave and open the door about a foot, expecting him to get lost.

"What are you waiting for?" He slides next to me then pushes the door wide with one arm, and eases me through with the other. The stench of body odour and sweaty laundry fill my nostrils. I cough. Sway from lightheadedness.

It's not that different from the girls' change room. Same yellow walls, chipping from age, and purple benches that line the room. There's nobody here except Carson, who looks like he's about to leave. He's a loud mouth from grade eleven. I barely know him but have heard all the rumours. He's the go-to guy for drugs and is known for being rough with his girlfriend. Fat Bastard is what I'd always called him behind his back. Carson looks at me, surprised. Doesn't say anything as he glances from me to Fitz, looking denser than driftwood.

"Oh, I'm sorry," I stand awkwardly. "I thought Stu was in here. I, uh, is he here?"

Carson shakes his head and frowns. "Nope. Left during the game. Puked on the field and went home."

"What?" I shift my eyes to Fitz. His arms are folded over his chest in front of the door, looking a little too Mount Rushmore for my comfort.

"Why did you tell me that..." I realize there's no point in finishing my sentence. He nods at Carson. A breath gets caught like a bug in my throat and I try to skirt around him, but he circles his arms around my back and pulls me into him.

"Hold her," Fitz instructs Carson, throwing me to him. My arms are flung behind my back.

"Let go of me!" I cry, but he pulls my arms tight into the centre of my back. I feel a snap somewhere in my left shoulder.

"Got some rope?" Carson asks.

"What?" I cry.

"It's a joke," Fitz laughs. "Although I kind of wish I did have rope. You'd like that, wouldn't you?"

"Kiss my ass," I say, trying to keep the tremor of fear out of my voice, but failing. Fitz pulls out his cell phone and flicks his thumb along the screen. Licks his lips. He lifts it so I can see my famous photo. I glance at it, and feel bile rising up my throat. My arms stretched above my head. Head turned slightly to the left, looking at the camera lens through the corners of my eyes. My breasts fully exposed. Nipples wide and dark like chocolate wafers. I'd always hated them. Shamefully big and unrefined. Like I'm part of a long lineage of nursemaids. I flash back to that night when I let him sneak in after mom and dad had gone to bed. Regret grips my heart for the thousandth time since he lifted his phone above me and snapped the photo. And, for the thousandth time, I wonder, how did I ever get into this awful mess? I look away.

"Not until I get some of this," he says.

"That's hot," says the dumb ass behind me.

"Stu will kill you when he finds out you did this." I decide to play the boyfriend card, whatever's left of it. Fitz lifts his hand to the top of my blouse and loosens the top button. Starts working on the next one.

"I doubt it," Fitz says, moving his mouth beside my ear. "He told me you guys are finished. And I can do whatever I want with you." As much as I'd come to despise Stu, my heart crumples that he could say something so callous.

"Get your hands off of me," I growl, catching the sob that almost escapes my throat.

"Relax Lana. We'll let you go in a minute," he answers. His hand rubs my left boob as nausea floods my stomach.

Fitz undoes another button and pulls my shirt wide so that my bra is showing. Stay calm, I tell myself, lest the window-shattering scream inside me bursts into all kinds of crazy. And, that's something that I cannot let happen. And give the fabbies more material for their slut campaign? No way.

I concentrate on the air going in and out of my nose. Some meditation technique I'd learned in yoga. *Keep your cool, Lana.* I think of cold things. Ice cream. Falling snow.

"Let go of me or I will scream," I say as calmly as I can muster.

"What the be-jeezus is going on here!" A man's voice rips into the room. We all turn at the same time to see the football coach standing with his legs apart, hands on hips, and lower lip jutting out like a shelf.

"Coach Diller!" Fitz jumps back. Carson drops my arms, freeing me to close my shirt.

"This isn't some by-the-hour hotel room! Get your girlfriend out of here."

He saves his most disgusted look for me and stomps to the exit. "You have thirty seconds!"

"Shit," Carson mutters as he grabs his things. "Think he'll call our parents? We could get kicked off the team for this."

"Relax, idiot. He's not going to do that. He wants us on the team. He knows we're just having fun."

"Fun?" I spit the word out, grab my bag and stomp toward the exit.

Fitz grabs my arm and smirks. "Next time we do photos."

I glare at him. Wish him dead. Wish he was as stupid as he looks. But he knows why I didn't scream. He knows I'll never tell a soul about this and risk adding kindling to the bonfire that is my life.

"Get your hands off me." I swing my palm back and slap Fitz across his face with the most satisfying sound I've heard in a while. "Don't you ever touch me again."

I rush from the room before Fitz breaks his stunned expression. The coach is outside the door, drinking a can of no-name soda. I glance at him, tempted to tell him that I was the victim in there. Maybe even say thank you for bringing it to an end. But his sneer tells me that would be a complete waste of time. That he knows as well as everyone else. Lana is a good-for-nothing whore.

I rush out of the school, stopping for a minute just beyond the school parking lot to pull out my phone. Tapping on my messages to Stu, I type what I hope will be my final text, ever, to him.

We. R. Finished. Asshole.

Chapter 6

Girl Unformulated

Mom is sitting at the kitchen table when I get home. Another long walk but, this time, not quite so therapeutic. Unless you call crying for thirty minutes therapy. So much for the theory on my twenty-minute limit.

"You're later than usual," Mom says as I hang up my jacket. Three red scented candles are lit in the hallway, forcing the smell of cinnamon through my nasal passages and causing me to cough. I look at my phone. Stu hasn't bothered to respond to my text.

"If I had a car, I would have gotten home a lot sooner." I step in front of the hallway mirror. The cheeks are a little blotchy, but my eyes are clear. I poof my hair and fake a smile at my reflection.

"I could have picked you up."

I enter the kitchen where she's sitting at the table, already in her pyjamas. Still in her pyjamas? A glass of red wine is next to her plate of shepherd's pie. Two place settings on either side of her.

"I didn't know I'd be so late," I reply, grabbing one of the empty plates from the table and helping myself to food.

"How was your day?" she asks.

"Pretty good." I sit down and grab the bottle of red sitting in the middle of the table and pour what's left into my own glass.

"Whoa!" Mom drops her fork. "What do you think you're doing?"

"Taking the edge off," I lift it to my lips and take two big gulps. Let it coat my throat with its bitter warmth. I don't know how people can enjoy this for its taste, but it's not so bad for the buzz.

"You shouldn't do that," Mom says. Rich, coming from her. Turning back to her own glass, she cradles it in her hands.

"Cheers." I raise my glass. She reluctantly clinks, unsmiling. She doesn't appear to be feeling any more celebratory than me, but in the world of family dysfunction, this is what passes for bonding. I imagine telling her about the photo. Her rising from the table and wrapping her arms around me, telling me it'll all be okay. That we'll get through this together. She scrapes her plate with the fork.

"Mom, do you ever feel like life is too much?"

"Too much? You're still worried about the money?" Stuffing the fork into her mouth.

"No. That's not it. I mean, what if you do something that you wish you hadn't. What if..."

"Everybody has regrets, honey. It's part of life." She takes a sip of wine and sits up suddenly. "Oh, I almost forgot. I bought you something for your complexion problem."

I shake my head. "I have a complexion problem?"

"I was at the mall today and told the woman at the makeup counter, you know the good ones in the department store, I told her about the pimples on your chin." She squints her eyes, leaning in to examine my face. "You look good now, though."

"I don't give a shit about my skin, Mom."

"You have such a foul mouth, Lana." She sighs. "I'm just trying to help, that's all. You're a pretty girl, but that goop you put on your face doesn't help you any. It's too oily. You should switch to powders."

"Yah." I drop my head and stare at the peas peeking through the slosh of ground beef and sauce. If she hadn't cut me off, I might have told her that nobody looks at my face except to aim something at it. I shovel the dinner into my mouth and push the chair from the table when I'm done. Mom doesn't like the truth. She wants pink balloons and silver confetti. Anything less will be dismissed. So, shut up and smile.

"It's by a new line of cosmetics. Fleur something. Want me to grab it now?" She asks, setting her hands on the table, about to lift herself up. I shake my head and rise.

"No." Dad is walking through the front door as I head upstairs.

"Lana," he says, "How was your day?"

"Fine." I stop midway up the steps and turn around. "I'm not feeling well tonight."

"Really?" He sets his hand on the banister. "If it's about the car..."

"No, it's not." I'm not going to help Mom lay all the blame on Dad. "I think I've come down with a stomach bug."

"All right. Let me or Mom know if you need anything, okay?"

Nodding my head, I continue to my room, shut the door behind me and pick up my cell phone. An argument erupts downstairs. Mom's voice is raised. Leveled responses from Dad, too muffled for me to make out his words. Not again. In need of a diversion, I send Demit a message.

Watcha doin?

I change out of my uniform, toss the blouse in the hamper and leave the kilt on the floor, then throw on a pair of track pants and a t-shirt. My phone dings.

DEMIT: Just hanging out. U?
LANA: Same. Shd start my english essay but not in the mood
DEMIT: I hear ya. Don't feel like homework either. How was football?
LANA: Boring. I left early
DEMIT: Were mean girls there?
LANA: Yep. In full form.
DEMIT: did u tell them off yet? >:o
LANA: No. Not yet
DEMIT: That's too bad. Hey! Feel like coming over? Sounds like you could use company
LANA: Not sure. Just told my parents I'm sick
DEMIT: r u?
LANA: No
DEMIT: Then come. Tell them u have to work on a project or something

I stare at my phone, not sure how to respond. I barely know this guy. It would be messed up to show up at his house, wouldn't it? I sigh. Laugh. What about my life isn't mess up these days? I really do need some company. I'm desperate actually. It might help get my mind off of Fitz, too.

LANA: All right. Better than hanging in my room
DEMIT: 177 Morrison Rd. C u soon
LANA: Cool. I can walk there. B there in 15

***

Three pink frosted cupcakes sit in the centre of a white plate. Demit's mother is standing across from me, her arms folded, examining my face.

"I know it's a lot, but if you just take one bite from each, that would be great." She has the same long, thin face as Demit, as well as his piercing stare. Even behind her black-rimmed glasses, I feel its penetrating scrutiny and press my arms into my sides to prevent myself from squirming.

Demit rests his hand on the back of my chair. "Mom, relax already."

I take a bite out of one and hastily nod my approval. "This is really yummy. What is it called again?"

"Cherry Ka-ching," she answers with a bright smile. "You like it?" I nod and move on to the next one, trying not to notice the dirty baking tins and bowls piled on the table around my plate.

"I can't believe you don't have a cupcake store here," his mom says, lifting a stack of dirty silver bowls from my left and adding them to the overflowing sink. "I'm going to just bake at home for starters, but there are a couple great locations I'm looking at to open a store."

Nodding, I taste the second cupcake which I recognize as salted caramel. It melts in my mouth. "This is awesome."

She lifts her shoulders and claps her hands, nodding her approval of my judgement. Moving on to the last one, I detect a weak peanut butter taste. The cake is crumbly.

"Yum," I raise my eyebrows and force a tight smile, fighting my gag reflex.

"You like it?" She points a finger at Demit. "See? It's not bad! I'll have to tell your sister, too. She's far too picky."

Demit knocks the back of my chair. "She's just being nice. We're going now. You've gotten your taste test, Mom." I push the chair back.

"Yes, you can go now," she waves us off as I follow Demit through a door that leads to a staircase downstairs. A girl walks into the kitchen, who I assume is Demit's sister, and complains about the mess. I only catch a glimpse of her, but she looks about fourteen. Tall and skinny, with coal black hair that hangs past her shoulders. An argument between her and her mom breaks out as we descend the stairs into a darkly lit room. Toward one end is a red couch, two old recliner chairs, and a flat screen TV. Empty pop cans and a rumpled bag of Doritos sit on a white coffee table. Clearly, housekeeping isn't a priority. My mom would have a heart attack if she saw this.

"Want a Coke?" Demit disappears into another room and re-enters with two cans.

"Thanks." I sit on the couch. "Your mom is interesting."

"If by interesting, you mean crazy, then yeah."

"Did she work in a bakery when you lived in Brooklyn?"

"No." He pauses, like he's thinking about what to say. "She was a magazine editor. Laid off last year. But she was sick of it by then and wanted to try something different. Like cupcakes. She's always loved to bake, so that's pretty much all she does these days."

"What magazine did she write for? Vogue? Elle?" I ask eagerly.

"World Financial Report," he says.

"Oh," I frown. "It must've been cool to live in New York City." Demit picks up a white electric guitar resting against one of the chairs.

"It was the best." He plays a couple of riffs.

"You play a lot?"

"Yeah. Do you know what this is?" He taps the face of the guitar.

"A guitar," I answer dryly.

"Not just any guitar. It's a Stratocaster. The one good thing that came out of my parents' break-up."

"Hmm. It looks cool. When did your parents separate?" He strums a soft tune that I don't recognize.

"Last year," he answers without looking up. "It was my dad's. He let me keep it when he moved to California."

"California?" I'm not sure if I've crossed the line from showing interest to prying, but after what I've been through today, I guess I don't care.

Demit sets the guitar back down and shrugs. "He got a job down there. That was the start of it. Quit his job as a professor when he landed a gig writing for a sitcom. That's when he told us he didn't want any of us moving with him. Not me or my sister. He needed time for himself, apparently."

"A sitcom?" I should have said something supportive, like wow, your dad really sucks. But divorce is so been-there, done-that. But writing for TV? Now, you don't hear that every day.

Demit strums his guitar for a minute. "Don't be too impressed. It's one of those annoying Disney sitcoms with the recycled jokes and canned laughter. Embarrassing, actually."

I cock my head and shrug. It's still TV. I shift my eyes to his arm tattoo.

"What's the tattoo say?"

"You can read it." He rises and sits close to me, stretching his arm out. I take his wrist in my hand, and follow the stream of words.

"Do I dare disturb the universe? In a minute there is time for decisions and revisions which a minute will reverse." It sounds profound, like I should nod my head gravely and respond with a deep observation. What I really want to do is read it again. Maybe two or three more times, so I can actually understand it.

"Didn't it hurt getting all of that tattooed?" I'm embarrassed that I can't come up with anything better to say.

Demit twists his arm to look at it. "It was worth it."

"Where's it from?"

"The Love Song of J. Alfred Prufrock," he says. "It's a poem by T.S. Eliot. I think you'd like it."

"I'm not all that into romance these days," I admit. He flips his head back and laughs. I'm not so much into feeling like an idiot either, I want to add.

"It's not romantic. It's about trying to fit in, loneliness."

"Hm. Sounds like my life."

"We're all lonely. The poem is a reminder to me to not get caught up in the need to fit in. At least that's how I read it." Demit rises from the sofa. He runs upstairs, returning a minute later, carrying a laptop. Resting it on the table in front of us, he sits back beside me. "Ever wish you could take control of your life? Stop letting everyone else decide who you are? There's freedom in not giving a shit about other people's opinions. Don't you think?"

I stare back at him, even as my thoughts wander to the locker room today. Fitz groping me. The coach eyeing me like I'm working the street. What is control? I'm wondering if I've ever experienced it. Can anyone, really?

"Yeah," I answer softly.

"To hell with them all," he says. "Nobody has any right to judge you."

I look at him from the corners of my eyes. "Yeah, right. That's a nice dream, but not realistic."

"When's the last time you disturbed the universe?" He asks, his eyes flashing. I cross my arms over my chest. This conversation is getting weird. Shrugging, I turn away and sigh, wishing I hadn't come after all.

"You don't deserve to be treated this way. No matter what you've done." His voice has turned soft. I suddenly feel hot.

"You know about it." I hunch forward, suddenly self-conscious. Laid bare. "You know about the photo."

"Yeah." He nods his head.

"You've seen it? Please tell me you haven't seen it."

He shakes his head. "No. Of course not. I found out through a guy I know and I read your Facebook page. I mean, it's out there. But it's not right how everyone has gone after you."

"You have no idea," I say.

"Then let me help you end it."

I laugh. "How do you plan to do that? Everybody hates me. What? Am I going to go all Carrie and burn the school down? Or go all Prom Night and kill everyone that has done me wrong?"

"All viable choices, but no." Demit lifts his laptop onto his thighs and flips it open. "Let's start with telling the world. You can't be the only person out there going through this kind of shit It's everywhere."

"What? Like a blog?" I chew my thumbnail. "I'm a terrible writer."

"Have you never read a blog? It has nothing to with writing ability. You're not writing the great American novel, you're just telling your own story."

Two thumbnails between my teeth now. Maybe he's onto something. What have I got to lose? My relationship with Stu is over and the fabbies show no sign of stopping their I-hate-Lana campaign. I think about all the humiliations I've suffered since the photo got out, fast forwarding to Fitz's attack today. Not sure I can share all that. Mostly, I want to erase it from my memory. Forget it ever happened, but somehow still keep the hate. Because I don't ever want to feel anything other than hate toward Fitz.

"I don't know about this. Who's going to care about my life?"

"Just start putting out there and see what happens." His elbow nudges my arm. "I care. And I think you'll see others do, too."

I stare at the dark television screen on the wall and nod my head. I guess I haven't anything to lose. "Okay. I'll try it."

"That-a-girl." He opens a new screen and gets to work. Fifteen minutes later, he has a website up. It's simple. White background with a picture of a graffiti covered school bus in the header. Across the top it reads, Girl Unformulated.

"How'd you come up with that?" I ask, pointing to the name.

Demit stretches out his arm. "I took it from a line in the poem. I know the eyes that fix you in a formulated phrase, and when I am formulated, sprawling on a pin, wriggling on the wall, then how should I begin to spit out the butt-ends of my ways." He shrugs. "Something like that, anyways."

"Wow." I wish I could better grasp what he just said, but I somehow feel the heaviness of its meaning. "Any other poems you can rhyme off from the top of your head?" I tease him.

"Just a few," he laughs. "I'm joking. That's the only poem I know, but shhh. Don't tell anyone."

I roll the name off my lips. "Girl Unformulated. It's pretty cool. Let's keep it."

"Awesome." He flips to another screen that looks like the back end of the website and passes the computer to me. "Time to write your first entry."

Chapter 7

The Power of One Plus One

October 8

The Photo That Killed Me

My senior year in high school. I had only one plan:
have a killer year. I had every reason to believe it
would happen:
  Hot boyfriend
  Super popular
  My own car
  Awesome BFFs
  Parties every weekend
  Sounds perfect, don't you think? No Plan B in
place. Why bother? I was on top of the world. Hell,
I felt like I owned the world. I mean, I kinda did. But

that was then and this is now. And now... I'm the most hated person at school.

Let me introduce myself. I'm Girl Unformulated. Call me GU, for short. Like Goo, which is kind of fitting since that's what you step on and later find stuck on the bottom of your shoe. Pretty much sums up my life. But how did it get this way? I'm about to tell you... or at least try. Welcome to my blog. It's the true story of my senior year, starting with how I went from popular to pariah in twenty-four hours.

Twitter version:

Boyfriend takes photo of girlfriend while fooling around. Shares photo with entire school. Girl loses all friends. Senior year hell.

Longer version:

He swore over his mother's grave that they were just for him. I really didn't see the harm in that. He was, after all, my boyfriend. I trusted him. And, anyways... It was just a photo and I wasn't the first girl to show her boobs to a camera. But mostly, I trusted him.

Word of caution: Don't ever trust ABF. This is worth repeating.

Don't ever trust ABF (Asshole Boyfriend.)

Fast forward to the next day. By lunchtime, I'm feeling a little paranoid. It seems like everybody is staring at me and whispering as I walk by. When

I see my BFF, she's kind enough to show me the photo (it was on her phone!) I'll spare you the details of what it looked like, but ugh! Who else had seen it? Apparently everyone.

I thought, at least, my BFFs would stand by my side. Surely, they wouldn't turn on me. How many of them had photos taken of them? Well, I was wrong. They turned their backs on me, except to call me a whore or slut. Suddenly everyone was in on the action. Slut, whore, skank, bitch... I heard it all. Every time I walked down the hallway, into a class, or across the school yard. My friends led the charge.

I figured this would all be forgotten in a few days and we'd be laughing about it in a week. But here I am, three weeks later, and still the most hated girl in school. No friends. No fun. No life. All because of one stupid photo? Seems crazy to me. There's got to be something more to this. But I can't figure out what it is.

At least one good thing has come of this. I finally broke up with my boyfriend. In other words: I am officially ON MY OWN. Translation: Total Loner. Mercy.

October 10

You Can't Get Past Spit

I know I promised to write the true story of my senior year from hell, but here's a little honesty for you. Some things I'm just not ready to share. I could go back to the very beginning and tell every awful incident that I've experienced but (a) that would probably get boring real fast, and (b) some stuff is just too humiliating for me to remember, much less write about.

So let's just start with the here and now. Because the way my life is going I still have plenty to tell you about! Like today, for instance, in English class. I am just so lucky to have two BFF's in that class. Even more awesome? They sit behind me. Oops, did I say BFF's, I mean BFH's. That's short for bitches from hell. Today one of them spat on my desk. WTF? Until today, I'd held out hope that we could eventually all be friends again. It was faint, but it was there. But there's something about spit. You can't get past saliva.

It all started with Abby (not her real name) creeping up behind me as I'm about to enter class and hissing in my ear. Made my stomach turn. At least she got one thing right. She is a snake. The stupid hiss got a good laugh from Sissy (the other BFH.) Sissy has no original thoughts in her head. She never has, which is why Abby loves her so much. Very monkey see, monkey do kind of friendship. Abby likes to control everyone and everything, so we've always had a patchy friendship. I never liked being on her leash. I imagine Abby dared Sissy to spit on my desk. And, voila. This made them both laugh hysterically. Sad, really. (Is this how I used to act?)

Halfway through class, they started up again. Balls of crumpled paper landing on my desk every few minutes. It took all my self-control to not turn around and slap them both. Instead, I tossed each ball into my desk. But the BFHs would not give up (they're good that way.) In a desperate act to stop them, I flattened one of the balls and read it.

WHY DON'T YOU DIE? BICH

Couldn't they at least have the intelligence to spell correctly? I raised my hand and asked the teacher if I could go to the office. Said I wasn't feeling well. When the teacher said okay, I left the paper lying on my desk for anyone to see (like, the teacher.) I heard Abby hiss (like the snake she is), "Grab it!" It almost made me smile.

English is last period, so I went to the office, faked a stomach ache and went home early. Just another day in the life of Goo. FML.

October 15

Top Ten Perks of Being a Loner

1. No need to freak out when a pimple shows up on your face. Nobody is looking at you anyway.
2. Pig out on chocolate guilt-free because you always "deserve it" after your day.

3. Spend hours of entertainment concocting methods of revenge.

4. Never pretend to say "that's sooo funny!" when a guy tells a lame joke. Nobody is talking to you.

5. Appreciate that one good friend is a thousand times more valuable than a thousand fake friends.

6. Never worry about being late. Nobody is waiting for you.

7. Discover you're pretty good company now that you spend more time with you than anyone else on the planet.

8. Finally memorize the lyrics to every song on your playlist.

9. Always get your way.

10. Never have to post "Gorgeous!" every time one of your GFs posts a new selfie

October 17

All you need is ONE

I have one friend left in my life. One. Friend. He is away today. Translation: not a single person talked to me all day.

If I'd never shown up, nobody would have noticed, hence I did not exist today. Do you know the saying, if a tree falls in the forest, but nobody hears it fall, does a tree really fall in the forest?

If a girl goes to school but nobody notices her there, does a girl really go to school? Does the girl really exist? I kinda wish I didn't exist. I'm not having any fun in this body. How about a restart button? Can I get one of those? There are a few things I would do differently if given the chance to start over:

1. Never pretend to like something that I don't
2. Ditch every friend that gossiped about me
3. Be nice to everyone, not just the ones who I think matter
4. Not care what others think of me
5. Stay away from boyfriends
6. Be unafraid to say how I really feel
7. Not obsess over my body and being skinny
8. Stay friends with most of the girls I ditched after grade 8. They were actually the nice ones.
9. Say how I really feel (yeah, this gets on the list twice.)
10. Not stay friends with Abby.

Maybe it's not too late to start over. Maybe today is the day I can flip the switch. But if I'm still treated like the old me, what's the difference? Is there any point? So many questions...

Life is hard.

Chapter 8

Cracked Reflection

"I want to shut down the blog," I say the second I settle into the seat beside Demit.

"Why? We've just started," he says, wiping his nose with his hand "You're getting traffic, you know. It always starts small, but at least people are reading it and commenting."

"It's not that. It's the fact that I'm depressing myself writing about my life. I thought it would feel good to get this off my chest but instead it's just a reminder of how shitty my life is, and how there's no end in sight! Where's my happy ending?"

Demit turns to look out the window.

"This is when you respond," I say. "It's called conversation, Demit."

He turns to look at me. "I'm thinking." I sigh. Demit thinks too much and too long. I'm trying to get used to his long silences in the middle of a conversation. It's hard not to take it personally. Like he's bored of the discussion and is hoping if he's silent long enough, I'll shut up and move on. And that kind of terrifies me. If Demit gives up on me, what do I have left? Nothing. I'm hanging onto him with all I've got. But that's a challenge in itself because I can never let him know how desperately I need him. That would make me pathetic.

"Maybe we need to ratchet things up for your blog," he finally says.

"What's that mean?"

"Do stuff. Show that we're fighting back. I mean, that you're fighting back. Give the readers a reason to cheer you on and feel empowered themselves."

I slowly nod, chewing the side of my tongue. "Okay, I'm listening. What do you suggest?"

"I have to think about it," Demit responds, staring intensely at me. "Am I allowed to think before I answer you?" He smiles.

"You're such a smartass. Let me know what your brilliant minds comes up with."

Demit nods. "I'm on it." He smiles, his beautiful blue eyes crinkling at the corners. I smile back.

"I'll meet you at your locker after last period," Demit says as the bus slows in front of the school. I agree, looking at his mouth and wonder how many girls he's kissed. Then I shake my head. The last thing I need is more drama in my life and everybody knows that love is the worst drama of all. Besides all that. We're just friends. We walk to the entrance together in silence, then wave good-bye, setting off in opposite directions. Dropping my head low, I walk toward my locker, dodging feet as I go.

"Good morning, Miss Tiller!" Mr. Zinsky calls out before I get very far. I wonder if he notices my cringe.

"Morning, Mr. Zinsky," I grumble, lifting my head to nod, but just barely slowing down.

"I hope you brought that good attitude with you today," he says, gripping his belt and pulling up the waistband of his pants.

"Yes, sir." My legs are twitching to run.

"Keep up the positive changes. She that wants the fruit, must climb the tree." I stare back at him and pretend to understand what he's talking about. I have my own line: *she who loses her friends, gains annoying principal.*

"Yes, sir." I nod, paralyzed on the spot until his unibrow relaxes and he shifts his eyes to another Sacred Heart victim. Mercifully, he abandons me. When I turn a corner, I almost fall into Mrs. Hendrickt. Although she's hard to miss in that mustard yellow blouse. It's an unflattering colour on anyone; even more so when you're obese.

"Lana!" She lifts her coffee cup to prevent it from spilling, then smiles. "You almost got me, there."

"Sorry Mrs. Hendrickt." I immediately regret my nasty thoughts. What happened to my rule to be nice? "I love your top," I say.

"Thank you! It's new." She almost blushes, which makes me feel even worse for lying. "I hope you're not trying to butter me up to gain brownie points for your essay mark?"

Shoot, I don't remember packing it this morning. The second she slips away, I drop my bag to the floor and rifle through it. I don't notice Alysa's boots beside me until I hear her voice.

"What the hell are you doing in my way?" she says sharply. Hatred winds into a tight ball in my chest. I don't look up. Nor do I respond. I just imagine scraping my nails into her cheeks.

"I'm talking to you," Alysa kicks my side. Not enough to hurt but enough to make me lose my balance and stumble onto my side. *If a girl falls in a hallway and everybody sees a girl fall in a hallway, does a girl wish she was dead?*

I lift my head. "I think there's plenty of space to walk around me," I respond without hiding the irritation in my voice.

"Oh God!" Alysa turns to someone behind me. "You've got to look at this, Fitz." All my limbs turn rigid. I'd been successfully avoiding Fitz since the locker incident, and can't bring myself to lift my gaze. His navy blue running shoes stop to the left of me.

"Look at what?"

"How ugly she is without makeup. I always said she needs makeup to look good. Now this proves it."

I can't take another second of this. Zipping up my bag, I rise from the floor and glare at her. "Bitch," I whisper.

Without any warning, Alysa presses her hands against my shoulders and shoves me against the wall. Presses her lips against my mouth as hard as she can before backing away.

"Who's the bitch now?" she asks, letting go of my shoulders. "Next time, wear some fucking lipstick." I stare at her. Unable to move. No thoughts can even rise to my consciousness to describe how I feel. Quickly, my glance skirts to either side of me. Students are staring. Not wearing looks of sympathy, but shame. Awful shame. I want to shrink so small that I can slide into one of the cracks in the linoleum floor and die.

"Holy shit! You did it," Fitz says, his mouth hanging open as he gapes at Alysa. "I only dared you as joke."

"Shut up," Alysa says as she drags him by the arm past me. Wiping my mouth with the back of my hand, I turn to spit her strawberry flavoured taste off of my lips. Then I watch her coast down the hallway where she catches up with Stu and knocks him on the shoulder. He turns and our eyes meet. I wonder if my gaze is as stone cold as his. Not even a skipped heartbeat. Nothing to indicate regret in my decision to break up with him. Shutting my eyes, I drop my chin and breathe deeply.

I am so fucking alone.

***

Being a library refugee has its benefits. On a really productive day, I get all my homework done before the day is out. A rarity, yes, but it's a step up from my pre-library days. Right now, I'm reading a snooze-worthy chapter on how Gutenberg's printing press spurred the Protestant Reformation. The thesaurus sits at the corner of my desk, beckoning me toward distraction, my latest novel on top of that. My head is growing heavy from boredom, dropping toward my chest every few minutes. A wooden desk, I've learned, is surprisingly comfortable when sleep beckons. Which brings me to another benefit of the library refugee system. Napping. Nothing will shame you for nodding off other than your own drool.

I shut the textbook and reach for my novel. A perk to living in Lonerville. I've rediscovered my love of books. And now am wondering why I gave them up in the first place. I picked out a Stephen King from a stack of old paperbacks in our basement, at home. It's not *Carrie*. I figured that might inspire too many ideas.

Last period starts in fifteen minutes, the dreaded English class with Sarah and Alysa. I never know what they'll do to me. After this morning's experience, I'm pleading the universe to be merciful and strike them both down with a crippling spell of the runs. Anything, really, to prevent them from attending class. My latest strategy of arriving early and reading at my desk until class begins seems to be working in my favour. Most days, they show up at the last second and don't have much time to harass me before the teacher gets going. I have to leave the library a few minutes before the bell rings to stick to the plan.

The halls are still empty as I rush past full classrooms. Passing the bathrooms, I realize I need to go, so turn around and head toward it.

"Lana," shouts a voice from behind me. My stomach twists when I see it's Fitz. I pick up my pace and push the door into the ladies' room. Five seconds later, it swings open behind me and before I have a chance to lock myself into a stall, two arms are gripping my waist.

"Let go!" I try to twist my body from him, but he holds tight.

"Anyone in here?" he asks as I squirm to break loose. When nobody responds, he pushes me into the first bathroom stall. I fall over the toilet as he slams the door shut and turns the lock. Spinning around, I swipe my hand at him, but he catches it before my finger nails slash his neck.

"Let me out of here," I hiss, panic pulsing so hard, I see red. He swings me around like I'm a sack of flour and smashes my back against the door, holding his hand over my mouth. I can't believe this is actually happening. I always knew Fitz was a creep, but never thought he was capable of this.

"Relax," he whispers. His hot breath blows into my ear. "We never got to finish what we started."

I shake my head and try to push him away but his chest is a brick wall. He pulls my shirt out of my kilt. I stifle a sob as his hand travels beneath it. The thought that he plans to rape me slams me into a state of shock. This can't really be happening.

"Leave me alone," I whimper.

"I'll be quick," he says gruffly, pulling his hand away and fumbling for something in his pocket. "Say cheese." The hairs at the back of my neck go rigid. He lifts his phone and takes a snapshot of me.

"Stop!" I free one of my arms and try to grab the phone from him, but miss. The phone drops to the floor and Fitz uses his free hand to tug at my underwear. The door to the bathroom opens. Two girls are laughing. I glance at Fitz. We have the same thought. I'm about to open my mouth to yell when he jams his palm so violently against my mouth that I feel my front teeth ache. I bite down on his flesh. He lets out a low groan. His eyes flash black.

"What the hell?" says one of the girls. They both giggle. Fitz and I lock eyes again. He drops his hand from my mouth and smiles triumphantly.

"Need some privacy?" Alysa laughs.

"A little constipation, perhaps?" Sarah adds.

My heart drops. He knows I can't cry out with them in here. Fuel Alysa's hatred of me? No thanks. She doesn't need another reason to accuse me of being a whore. A boyfriend thief. I rest the back of my head against the stall door and close my eyes. Concentrate on the air moving in and out of my chest while Fitz lifts my skirt and rubs his hand between my legs.

"He told me he tried breaking up with her weeks ago," Alysa says all cloak-and-dagger. "He just didn't want to hurt her feelings. She's so needy, right?"

"Stu's too good for her," Sarah adds.

"She threw herself at him. Right from the start. Of course he went out with her. But eventually that wears off."

My stomach is in knots listening to this while Fitz reaches deeper inside of me. I truly, completely wish I was dead. Head pounding, I hold my breath as Fitz breathes heavily into my face. I tell myself I don't exist. If I don't exist none of this is happening.

"Now we get to see that rat in English," says Sarah.

"God, I've hated her for so long. It's about time her perfect life turns to shit, isn't it?" Alysa laughs as their shoes shuffle out the door. My chest is about to explode when I realize I've been holding my breath since they started talking. I barely register that Fitz has pulled his hand away. With my ears ringing from what I've just heard, I feel like I've been beaten and battered for hours. In fact, my mind can barely register what has just happened. Yes, Fitz raped me. I think. Didn't he? But it also felt like my girlfriends raped me too. Like my entire worth was yanked from my inside and slopped to the floor. How long has my best friend hated me? How could I have not known it?

"I've got to get to class. I have a test today," Fitz mutters, as he opens the stall door and turns to look at me.

"Just get out," I say, leaning into the corner of the stall.

"Like you didn't enjoy that." He snorts. I hear him shuffle out of the washroom.

I don't know how long I leaned there, my head resting against the wall. By the time I reach for my phone, I see I'm now fifteen minutes late for class. I need to gather my things and pull myself together. I don't want someone to find me like this. Standing upright, I tuck in my shirt and retrieve my books from the floor. I see Fitz's cell phone on the floor and a jolt of adrenaline courses through me.

Picking it up, I rub my finger across the screen. Passcode. *Damn.* Tossing it into my bag, I leave the stall. I can't think straight. My head feels like a thick dark void.

Standing in front of the mirror, I flatten my hands over my hair, move strands back into place. Alysa's words race through my mind. *God, I've hated her for so long.* I feel like if ever there was a good excuse to cry, this would be it. Weird, though. My pupils are dry as sand. Maybe I'm in shock. Isn't that some sort of medical condition that freezes your thoughts, or something? Or maybe I'm not as surprised as I should be. Alysa and I have always competed with one another. Sometimes she won, sometimes I won. Sometimes I was the skinniest. Sometimes she had the most expensive clothes. She always got better marks. I guess I always got the cuter guy. To me, it was a fair trade-off. But to her? An uber-competitive type-A personality with psycho parents who set impossible standards? Maybe she had to win at everything. Maybe losing to me in anything was enough to set her hatred on fire. And, maybe my photo was the one thing that could give her the edge she always wanted over me. I sneer at my reflection, imagining myself looking at her. "Fucking bitch," I say, wishing it was to her face.

I imagine Fitz's smug face and something inside of me snaps. I can almost hear it. A slight zing that compels me to tear my bag from my shoulder and smash it into the mirror.

"Fucking asshole!" The mirror cracks, but mercifully does not shatter. I swallow a breath, terrified by my rage. *How messed up am I?* Exhale and thank God the mirror didn't shatter. Thank God the reflection is still intact although cracked. A fitting reflection of the girl looking at it.

With a shake of my head, I button up my blouse, noticing the black bra showing through the white cotton. I try to remember the last time I wore a white bra. A stupid thought, I know. Who cares? What does it matter what colour my bra is? It nags at me as I leave the bathroom and head for class. When's the last time I wore a plain white bra. Grade nine? Grade eight? Definitely before I gave much thought to boys. I decide in that minute that I'm wearing white bras from now on. For some reason, this small goal delivers me a sliver of peace.

Thankfully, Mrs. Laccetta is away and the supply teacher looks like he's as anxious for the day to end as we are. He waves at me from the back of the class where his feet are propped up on the desk.

"We're having individual study right now," he says, taking a sip from a can of Coke. "Your teacher says you all have an assignment to work on, so use your time wisely."

I nod, pull out my copy of 1984 and start reading where I last left off. My chair is shoved from behind. I ignore it. Another shove. Alysa's foot. I'd like to turn around and yank her ankle so hard that she flies to the floor and lands on her fat rear end. Instead, I twist my body to glare at her.

"What?"

Alysa and Sarah exchange smiles then look back at me with matching sneers.

"How's it feel to be the biggest loser in the school? Now that you don't have Stu to prop you up, you're nothing," says Alysa.

Alysa's big silver hoops sway as she turns to smile at Sarah, then fixes her stare back onto me. She's wearing the hairband I helped her pick out this summer. A wide white one with yellow polka dots. I have the same one in pink. Mirror images, the two of us. *Pathetic.*

I roll my eyes and return to my book, but the words don't register meaning. A storm of anger is brewing in my head. When was the last time I got dressed without thinking about who would see me? And, why the hell should I care so much about what others think? Particularly those who have a keen interest in hating me. I need a change. No. I need to change. I sense something like a window opening inside my mind. As though a whiff of fresh air is circulating in my brain, unsettling the dust, clearing the stuffiness. Is this what it feels like to have a revelation?

I'm not a hundred percent sure what my big a-ha is. It's not like I experience outbursts of brilliance very often. Well, never. But I know it has something to do with me and change. Not the kind of change that is forced on me. God knows I've had enough of that. I need to instigate the change. I've made it too easy for them to go after me. They know how desperately I've wanted back in with the fabbies. Not anymore. It's like something has finally snapped out of place. Or into place? I think of Fitz's phone sitting in my bag. I'm sick of being the victim. It would be nice to play the predator. I walk to the back of the class where the supply teacher is half-asleep. He looks at me through one open eye.

"Yes?"

"May I go to the bathroom?" I ask. He waves me off and returns to his slumber. It's time to put my hatred to use.

Chapter 9

Smashing Success

A custodian storage room is conveniently located across from the women's bathroom. I take a quick peek inside. It's empty. Slipping in, I almost trip over a mop resting against the door frame. There have got to be tools in here somewhere. Paper towels, garbage bags, cleaning sprays. I scan the shelf on the opposite side of the room, and zero in on a hammer hanging beside some kind of levelling tool and paint brushes. Perfect. Grabbing it, I scoot out of the room and cross the empty hallway into the bathroom.

I glance at the stall where Fitz just attacked me and my knees grow weak. Purposely, I don't look at the mirror. Setting the phone and hammer onto the counter, I steady myself and close my eyes. Take a deep breath. No revenge is severe enough to make up for what he did to me, but this is a start. My own phone vibrates in my cardigan pocket. Demit.

DEMIT: Getting out of school early today. Meet at my place later?
LANA: OMG! This is perfect!! I'm in girls bathroom on first floor. Meet me here!! Hurry!!
DEMIT: The girls bathroom? R u joking?
LANA: No. I'm serious. I need ur brainiac help. Just meet me in here. Im alone. Hurry!!
DEMIT: Ok. B there in a minute. U better b sure no one else is there.
LANA: Just hurry!

A minute later, there's a knock at the bathroom door. I swing it open and pull Demit in by the wrist. He looks around in awe.

"Geez, it's so clean," he says. "Light blue? I always thought the floor was beige. Wait a sec. What happened to the mirror?"

"Forget about that." I pick up Fitz's phone. "Can you hack this?" Demit raises an eyebrow.

"Whose is it?"

"An asshole's. Now can you hack it or not?" Time is ticking and I need to act fast. He moves his gaze to the hammer and back to the phone.

"You want to tell me what's going on?"

I sigh. "I will, honest. But I need you to trust me right now because we don't have much time." I growl, rubbing my hand over my face. *Fuck. Fuck. Fuck.* "I shouldn't have asked you to come. I don't know what I'm doing." I feel myself chickening out. Maybe I should just toss the phone in the toilet and be done with it. My glance rests on the crack in the mirror and my stomach grinds.

Demit lifts his hand up. "All right. I trust you." He takes the phone and presses the home button. "The easiest way to hack is to just guess the password. We have six chances. I assume this is Stu's phone? What's his birthday?"

"It's not Stu's," I answer. His stare is unnerving, but I don't flinch.

"Okay. Do you know this asshole's birthday?"

"No," I bite my thumbnail. "But I know what number is on his football jersey. Would that help?"

Demit wobbles his head. "Sure. Let's give that a try. What is it?"

"Twenty-three."

Demit types in two different number combinations then shakes his head.

"I know he celebrated his birthday in the summer. Does that help?"

Demit sighs. "Maybe twenty-three is the day of his birthday." He shrugs. "It's worth a try but if this doesn't work, I know one other way to hack an iPhone but it doesn't always work."

He tries a couple more numbers. "Got it! Oh-eight-twenty-three. He's an August baby. That's just plain ass good luck." He hands the phone to me. "Now what?"

I open the phone's camera roll and find my picture. It's really not that indecent, but I look like a crazed witch. Definitely not a photo I want shared. *Delete*. I tap onto his message app and think for a few seconds before typing *I'm a pig*.

Demit looks over my shoulder. "That's all sorts of lame. Are you trying to destroy this guy, or what?"

I flip my eyes to him. "You got something better?"

"Oh yeah," he holds out his hand and I drop the phone into it. "This guy's a real asshole, right?"

"The worst."

He types in something then holds it out for me to see.
My mom gives me the best blow jobs

I half-cough, half-laugh. "Oh shit. Really?"

"Too strong?" Demit asks. My stomach is a pretzel of nerves as I select *All Contacts.*

"Nah."

"You sure you want to do this?" Demit asks. My finger hovers over *Send.* I tap it. And, the text is gone. Popping up on screens across the school, probably across the city. I cringe to think his parents will read it, but he deserves all the suffering I can inflict on him.

"What do you want to do with the phone?" Demit asks, looking at the hammer. I had only planned to use it as a last resort. If I couldn't delete the picture. I pick up the hammer to return to the custodian's room. Then have a sudden change of heart. Dropping the phone to the floor, I lower to my knees and raise the hammer over my head. Smash it against the glass screen with all my might. Once. Twice. Three times. Each blow releasing a bit of the anger gripping my heart.

"Whoa," Demit breathes. "That is one dead fucker."

I gather the shattered pieces into my hands and drop everything into a tampon disposal box inside a stall. No guy will ever look in one of those.

"I need to get back to class," I announce, dropping my own phone back into my pocket. I try not to think about what Fitz will do to me if he ever figures out what I've done, shuddering at the possibilities. It was worth it, I decide. This victim gig is really wearing on me, and I'm ready to fight back. I think.

Demit looks at his watch. "Twenty minutes left. I'll return the hammer for you. Was it in the custodian room?" I nod as he rests his hand on my shoulder. "See you later?"

"Sure." He rushes out of the bathroom, leaving me, flushed with adrenaline. My heart is still racing. I feel triumphant. For a second I consider what Fitz will do to me when he puts the pieces together, but just as quickly push that from my mind. I'm going to enjoy this experience for as long as I am able.

***

I look at my watch sitting on the counter as I get out of the shower to towel off. Demit will be here in a couple hours. Scrubbing myself of Fitz's handprints was the first thing I did when I got home. I feel a bit better, but not really. I don't know if anything can erase the feelings of disgust that run through my veins. Trying to stop the replay in my mind, I think about Fitz's phone. I wish I could feel the same satisfaction just from the memory. But I don't. It's not enough. I want him to suffer infinitely for what he did to me. I wonder if he knows about the text yet. If he's experienced any fallout. And, what he'll do to me if he realizes I did it. He can't possibly do anything worse than what he's already done. Can he?

Mom is working the evening shift at the store today, so I don't expect to see her before nine-thirty. As if on cue, I get a text from her.

MOM: Will b late tonight. Cook a frozen pizza for din
LANA: How abt delivery
MOM: No. Dad bought frozen pizzas. Cook one

I'm impressed Mom is actually heeding Dad's advice, for once. As I head downstairs, I hear the TV playing in the living room. Tinny sounds of girls screeching at each other.

A reality show. Which is really a stupid word to describe these programs. Everyone knows they're the opposite of reality. Everyone is acting. Acting like they're not acting. Working the screen to come out the hero of the show. Trying not to be the one most harshly judged who ends up on the cover of In Touch magazine with a dimpled ass in a thong under the headline **Guess Whose Butt!**

I can barely handle being jerked around by my BFFs. Pleasing thousands of viewers at once? That's got to be tough. Unless you're the favourite. Adored by fans. I wonder how I'd pan out. I like to think I'd be loved. Today's phone smashing would have made great TV drama. Send ratings through the roof. Made me a star.

It's best I don't think about Fitz anymore. Put it out of my mind. Tell myself it was just sex. Horrible, unwanted sex. Leave it at that. Better to not admit what it really was. The big R word. Better not say that too openly. When one of the fabbies accused her ex-boyfriend of the big R last year, we all sided with her ex. She switched to a private school the next year. Not one of my proudest moments.

Despite my efforts to rid my head of the memory, I find myself in front of my laptop opening up my blog. I don't even know what I'm going to write but somehow the words flow.

October 18

The hate is growing

I was attacked today. Yes it was a physical attack, but I don't think that's what was the

---

worst part about it. I feel like he assaulted my soul. Scrunched it tight into a little ball of garbage and threw it aside.

Yes. It. I am an "it" today. A thing to him. Well, to all of them. They can't possibly think of me as human. If they did, they wouldn't be so cruel. Would they? Every day, I'm reminded of how insignificant I am. Just a toy for them to get their sick kicks with. I don't know how much more I can take of this. Today's attack has pushed me to a new low. I may be small but my hate is growing. They say whatever doesn't kill you makes you stronger. I don't feel strong. Does that mean this is killing me? I. Want. To. Die.

I don't read it over. Just click publish and smack my laptop closed. Maybe it will be the last post I ever publish. Maybe today will be the day I slit my wrists. I drop my head on my laptop and cry until I can barely catch my breath. I stuff my face into my pillow and feel the fabric turn wet.

When I finally stop crying, I realize something. I'm not ready to give up yet. Not tonight, anyways. They haven't broken me completely. I won't go down without a fight. And, besides all that, Demit is coming over tonight. A small relief from my pain and loneliness.

Demit arrives earlier than expected.

"Hey," I open the door to let him in past me.

"Oh." He stands awkwardly with one hand behind his back.

"Are you coming in?" I'm shivering from the chilly air rushing through the doorway.

He's not looking me in the eyes like he normally does. If I didn't know him so well, I'd think he was acting shy.

"What are you doing?" I ask, looking at his arm tucked behind his back.

"What do you mean?"

"Are you hiding something? What's behind your back?" I lean over to see.

"It's just a little something." He swings his arm around, pulling out a small bouquet of white and yellow flowers.

"What the..." I raise my eyebrows. "Flowers?"

His face grows pink. "Yes, they're flowers. No, I did not buy them. My mom got them from a client today and when I told her I was coming to your house, she said I should bring them to you. Our house is such a disaster from the cupcakes that she has nowhere to put them."

"So, you're giving me your mom's flowers?" I ask, but I'm joking. It's very sweet.

"Well, I told my mom you had a rough day. So, she insisted I bring them. I know. Stupid." He drops them to his side.

I smile. "Nobody has ever brought me flowers before. So, thank you." I extend my hand and Demit hands them to me, shrugging.

"It's freezing. Come on in." He steps inside the house and looks around.

"It smells like apple pie or something. You baking?" he asks.

"No. It's one of those fake scented plug-ins. Our house always reeks."

He coughs. "Smells good." I enter the kitchen to fill a vase with water.

I hear him flick his shoes off as I'm pushing the flowers into the glass vase.

"You want a drink?"

"Sure. I'll have a Coke. Or whatever you got that's closest."

I open the refrigerator. "Tomato juice or chocolate milk."

"Chocolate milk."

After pouring two tall glasses of milk and stirring syrup in them, I flip open my parents' liquor cupboard. Pull out a dark brown bottle and read the label.

"Want some Baileys? I think we earned it today." Demit grimaces. I don't wait for his answer and pour a generous shot into each glass.

"Cheers," he says with shrug. "To GU." We clink and drink. Mom won't be home for awhile yet, so I grab the bottle. It's Friday and I'd like to forget my life.

"Let's go upstairs." Demit follows me into my bedroom. I grab my laptop and sit cross-legged on my bed, leaning against the pillow and cradling my drink. Turning on a playlist, I look for a song to play. I don't know indie music like Demit, so I settle on a retro eighties song for now. Demit looks at my bed, then at the chair beside my desk. Clearly at odds with where he should park himself. Sizing up Demit's tall lean frame, I wonder what it would be like to lie beside him. His lips against mine. I flick it out of my head like a pesky bug. Maybe bringing him up here was a bad idea. Me and guys and bedrooms are not a healthy mix. And, besides all that, Demit and I are just friends. I'm about to get up when Demit flops down next to me, his knee touching mine.

"Today was crazy," he says, waiting for me to elaborate. But I don't feel like sharing right now. I let the pause stretch until awkwardness sets in.

"You don't need to tell me about it." He nudges himself an inch away from me. "But it'd be all sorts of awesome for your blog to tell your fans the shit you disturbed today."

"I don't know." I twist hair around my finger and avoid his gaze. Clearly, he hasn't seen my last post.

"I know you don't want to talk about it, but what do you think will happen if this guy finds out it's you?" Concern creeps into his voice.

"It'll be fine." I say lightly. "He'll never find out." I don't want to admit that the thought freaks me out a little. *He can't possibly do anything worse than what he's already done. Can he?* I finish up my glass of milk.

"More?" I ask, leaning over the side of my bed to pick up the bottle. Demit's glass is still a quarter full, but he shrugs and offers me his glass anyways. Pouring liquor into his, and then mine, I take a slow, lazy sip. Demit turns to his phone. Texting. Playing a game. Whatever. I close my eyes and listen to the music. Let my head float like a parachute.

"What're you thinking about?" Demit asks after a while. My eyes flutter open. His usually intense gaze is soft and out of focus. A half-smile on his face. Our knees are touching again.

"Freedom," I say.

"Freedom's good. From what?" He drops his phone onto the carpet and leans one hand on the bed. My mind drifts until Demit tugs my big toe. "Hello? Earth to Lana."

"Freedom from caring about anyone and anything. Freedom from judgement," I say, swiping his hand away from my foot. "That tickles."

"Maybe it's easier than you think," he suggests, resting his hand on my knee and sending a warm shiver up my thigh.

"Nothing is easy when it comes to my life. What I need is an enormous eraser to make the last month of my life disappear." I stop. Close my eyes and shake my head. "The same thought keeps coming back to me. That I brought all of this hell on myself. Things don't just happen for no reason."

"That's crazy to blame yourself."

"Is it?" I pull my knees into my chest and hug them. "I don't think so. You know I used to love school? All through elementary school, middle school. And, by grade ten I was practically failing half my classes. Chasing boys. Sometimes I think the insults hurt so much because maybe they're true."

"You need to stop telling yourself that." Demit shakes his head. "So what happened? How did you go from smarty-pants to failing?"

"Matching headbands." I think about Alysa's perfect hair. How struck I was by our mirror images today in class. "Being popular is hard work. The hair. The clothes. Getting the guy. Hell, getting every guy. Losing a bit of myself with every effort. Having a mom who can never let me forget how perfect she once was. Who cares more about my complexion than my marks." I sigh, feeling my inner drama queen surface. "I'm rambling."

Demit's toque has slipped back on his head. A few curls have fallen to the side of his forehead. His blue eyes gaze at me. "What do you want now?"

I search for an answer. What do I want? My head floats. "I'm tired. I want out. I think I can honestly say I just don't give a shit about anything anymore. Is that bad?" I lean my head back against the wall and look up at the ceiling. Notice a thread of web stretching from one end of my light fixture to the next. "Why can't they all just leave me alone?"

"What if we changed the rules?" Demit asks, standing up. He moves to the chair at my desk and wheels it to the edge of the bed, facing me.

"What do you mean?"

"You're still following the same rules. Waiting for them to free you. But they're stuck in the same game, too. Get it? As long as they believe you want back in, they can control you. We have to show them that you're breaking ranks."

I'm mesmerized by his hypnotic voice. His crazy ideas. "What do you want me to do now?" I ask, dropping my legs off the bed, setting a hand on his knee. Breathing in his presence.

"It's not what I want, Lana." Demit covers my hand with his palm. It's warm. Nice. "It's what you want."

"How do you become the complete opposite of yourself? That's what I have to do."

"What you want is to be true to yourself. Maybe go over-the-top at first. Make a big impression, right? Show them you're done."

"Like wiping the slate clean? Starting all over?" My mind is awhirl. I don't know where to start. I can't just reverse three years and go back to who I was. That girl is gone, too.

"Don't worry about where you end and where you start. Just be." Demit sucks back the last of his drink. "Each of us creates our own reality based on what we think is true. Change your thoughts, change your life. You know?" Raising his empty glass into the air, he says, "Be whoever the hell you want to be."

I hiccup and we clink.

"I wouldn't even know where to start," I say. "How about bra burning?"

"You're about fifty years too late. But I'm all for going bra-less," Demit smiles.

"Well, that's not exactly what I meant." Jumping off my bed, I open my underwear drawer. Pull out all of my fancy push-up bras, one by one. Red and black, polk-dot, fuschia with black bows. Into the garbage pail. Grab all the thongs and add them, too. Panty-lines be damned, I was not going to suffer another moment of perma-wedge.

"That seemed pretty anti-climactic," I announce. "Now what?" I've purged myself of two-thirds of my underwear. Not exactly a Lana revolution. I laugh at my pathetic attempt to re-make myself. This is all I can come up with? Demit studies me from his chair, an amused look on his face. I look in the mirror over my dresser. Photos of me and my BFFs taped along the sides. Matching smiles, yoga pants, and blonde highlights. Running my fingers through my long hair, I wonder if I can do what I'm thinking.

"I might need some help with this," I say, motioning Demit to follow me. In my parent's bathroom, I open the cupboard under the sink and rifle around until I find them. Mom bought a few Clairol colour kits last weekend. Big sale at the drug store.

"Not sure it'll be as Nice 'n Easy as it says," I say, holding up the box of hair colour. The model's hair looks brown with a touch of red. "Natural medium auburn," I read. "What do you think?" I hand it to Demit and turn to the mirror.

"I say go for it." Demit stares back at me through the reflection.

"I'll need two boxes for all this hair." My blonde hair drapes to the top of my shoulders. I know I won't look as pretty without my blonde hair. It's a depressing thought, but I ignore it.

"You said you wanted to change," Demit breaks through my thoughts.

"You're right." I clutch the counter for a minute while I wait for my head to stop spinning. The booze has kicked in. "This is big. I've been a blonde since grade nine. Barbie."

"Barbie's a ho." Demit says matter-of-fact.

"Nice," I roll my eyes. "I used to play with barbies, you know."

"Start the brainwashing early." I'm sure he's joking, but he makes a good point. "You could always dye it back if you don't like it, right?"

I open the box and empty the contents onto the counter. "Yeah, dye it back." It sounds like a sensible backup plan. Steadying myself against the counter, I squint at my reflection. Last look at the blonde girl.

"Time for change," I announce, pulling my sweatshirt over my head and immersing my hair under the running faucet. Once my head is soaked, Demit pulls a towel from the rack and hands it to me.

"Did you read the directions?" I ask. A large white sheet is unfolded beside the sink. Demit is wearing the clear plastic gloves that come with the kit.

"Are you gay?" I ask. I'm sorry I say it the second the question comes out of my mouth but he's standing in a pink t-shirt wearing plastic gloves and holding a bottle of hair colour. "I mean. Not that it matters."

Demit's mouth drops open. "Really?" He lifts the bottle into the air. "No, I'm not gay. Now comb your hair so I can rub this colour in."

Chapter 10

Not Alone Anymore

The damage is done. I'm blow drying my hair and it's looking more red than brown. Pink, actually. And not a pretty pink. A mix between cotton candy and jack-o-lantern. I'd stupidly lost track of time picking out music with Demit and left the dye in an extra 10 minutes. Okay, maybe 15 minutes.

"I think it looks good," Demit says.

"Easy for you to say. It's not on your head," I snap. Taking a deep breath through my nose, I slowly exhale. Try to get used to the girl in the mirror. "I look like a freak." I turn the blow dryer off and brush my hair. Already missing my blonde locks. What was I thinking?

"I don't look anything like myself anymore."

"Isn't that the point?" Demit asks cautiously.

I look at him. Searching for a sign that he's just trying to make me feel better. But his straight face doesn't betray that. I guess he's sort of right. I stare at my reflection and scrutinize the girl looking back at me. Maybe she looks a little cool. I take an elastic band out of a drawer and pull my hair into a ponytail. It tames the look a bit. Standing taller, I pose for the mirror.

"You don't mind it," Demit says. I shrug. It's too late now to do much about it.

"I'll get used to it. Eventually." I have to admit, I can appreciate feeling like someone other than myself. Like I'm playing dress-up. I wonder if I can pull this off come Monday. My stomach turns thinking about it.

We return to my room and flop down on the bed. Somehow, I end up resting my head on his chest listening to his heart gently beating. He's playing with my ponytail. A distant voice reminds me we're just friends, although at this moment, that feels fuzzy.

"What's next?" I ask. My phone rings before he can respond. Lifting myself from the bed, I answer it.

"Hello?"

"Hi Lana." My mom's voice is chirpy on the other end. "I'll be a touch later than I'd planned. Kerry has asked me to work out some inventory issues before I go."

"Okay, Mom," I answer. Demit pokes me in the ribs and I break out in a giggle.

"What are you doing?" Mom asks.

I look at Demit and put a finger to my lips. "Say hi to your mom," he says loud enough for her to hear.

"Is there a boy there?" Mom asks. "Is it Stu?"

"No. I mean, yes. There is a boy. And, no. It's not Stu."

"I don't want strange boys in our house when Dad and I are not there, Lana."

"Well, he certainly is a strange boy, but he's just a friend," I say, emphasizing the last word.

"Does Stu know about this?"

"Oh Mom! Stu's a douche." Demit doubles over laughing.

"Lana, watch your language."

"We broke up, Mom."

There's silence on the other line. "I gotta go, Mom. I have a *friend* here. See you later, okay?"

"Please stay out of trouble, Lana."

"Yes, Mom. Bye, Mom." I pick up the bottle of liquor and shake it. Empty.

"Will they notice it's finished?" Demit asks as I'm heading out of the room.

I shrug. "Probably not. Mom's too drunk half the time to notice anything. And Dad's a lot more concerned about Mom's drinking habits than mine."

"Your mom drinks a lot?" Demit asks.

I shrug. "Yeah. I mean, she hides it all right. It's not like she's stumbling around the neighbourhood with a bottle in a paper bag. She just drinks a lot of wine mostly. Passes out on the couch a lot. Burns dinner. That sort of thing. It's mostly annoying. How about you? Your mom a dead beat?"

Demit shakes his head. "Not really. My mom's gone all holy roller since Dad left. Church every Sunday. Lights Jesus candles. Just bought some stone statue of Buddha for our garden. Mid-life crisis, I guess."

"Pfff." I roll my eyes. "I think I'd rather have a boozer."

Demit shrugs. "It's not so bad. Better than her crying every night, which is what she did after Dad left. Now that she's got her cupcakes and bible, she's doing a lot better." He stands up and stretches his arms over his head. "What's with all the BFF pics on your mirror? I thought you hated all these girls."

"I don't want my mom to get suspicious. As soon as I trash them, she'll start asking questions. It would kill her to learn I'm not miss popularity anymore. That shit means the world to her."

"That's too bad," Demit mutters as he picks up an old snow globe of the Eiffel tower sitting on my dresser, and shakes it. When he puts it down, he looks at his phone and gasps. "I've got to go! I didn't realize how late it was. My mom just texted me. I was supposed to be home by now and she's ticked."

"Aw." I don't hide my disappointment.

"Write up your post tonight, ok?" I nod as he races out of my bedroom. I follow him down the stairs where he grabs his jacket and stops, one hand on the door knob.

"I'll see you tomorrow" he says, staring intently at me. For a second, I think he's going to lean over to kiss me. His face is only inches away. But he doesn't. My buzz is turning to a headache, anyways. I need a nap.

"Meet at the coffee shop in the morning?" He asks as he steps outside. I agree, then watch him walk down the driveway before finally closing the door. Mom will be home in about an hour, so I better get that pizza cooked. I wonder how she'll react to my new look. Change that. I wonder how seriously she'll flip her lid. How hard she'll beg to take me to the salon to fix it.

With the pizza in the oven, I decide to lie on the couch. My phone rests on my chest. Demit has already texted me three times to tell me how awesome I look. Every time, it makes me smile. I eventually doze off, waking up when I hear a loud bang. Something falling? Or was I just dreaming? Holding my breath, I listen for a few seconds. Nothing. Probably something fell in a cupboard somewhere. I close my eyes again when another text dings. I lift it into the air to read it. Every muscle in my body tenses. Although it's from an unknown number, I immediately know it's Fitz.

U little bich. I know u did it
I want my phone back. Tonight

My heart jumps into my throat. Did I lock the front door after Demit left? Springing off the couch, I run into the hallway. The bolt is locked. A sigh of relief. I'm being paranoid. Shaking my head, I send Demit a text to tell him about Fitz's message.

He knows

A new text pops up as I hit send.

I'm here

A tremor races across my neck. I look around the hallway, and quietly step across the floor into the kitchen. Looking carefully around me. This is ridiculous, I realize. I let my shoulders drop and laugh, shaking my head. He's bluffing. Turning around, I walk back into the hallway to grab my school bag when suddenly, Fitz steps out of the living room and into the front hallway. I scream, then slap my lips shut.

"Fitz. What the hell? You scared the heck out of me." I clutch my chest and breathe deeply. Hope that I'm not looking as terrified as I feel.

Stepping backward, I slowly inch into the laundry room. Should I make a run for it? Every cell in my body is telling me *yes*. But I don't. Take a breath. Keep cool.

"Surprise," he says, following me into the laundry room, cluttered with coats and shoes. Beneath his red baseball cap, his eyes glisten with determination. He shuts the door behind him, leans his hand against the counter not far from a stack of my mom's neatly folded underwear and a pile of unmatched socks. I feel oddly embarrassed for her, like it's an unnecessary invasion of my mom's privacy. My hatred for him grows.

"Orange hair?" Fitz snickers. "That's an interesting look."

"I don't have it." I stand firm, trying not to betray the terror I feel but my voice is trembling. "And you shouldn't be in here! You're breaking and entering. I'm calling the police." I don't remember where I left my phone. Is it in the kitchen?

"You're funny, Lana. Pretending you didn't do it. Very cute." He scratches his jaw with a scowl. I hear the slight grating of stubble against his fingers. "I dropped the phone in the bathroom. By the time I realized it was still there, I was in class and the test had started. There was no way for me to get it until school was out. But funny enough, before I'd even had a chance to find it, people were giving me all these weird looks as I left the classroom and walked down the hallway. Making stupid comments about me and my mom, who by the way, got the text too."

"I didn't send that text. I swear." I back into the laundry room door that leads outside. With my hand behind me, I turn the lock slowly and twist the knob.

"You sent the text." He grabs my arm, pulls me tight against him and stabs his finger into my chest. "Admit it."

"You're hurting me," I try to loosen my arm. "Let me go and I'll tell you."

He drops my arm and folds his arms in front of his chest.

"I did it." My voice is surprisingly hard. "What did you expect me to do? You drag me into the bathroom and do what you want with me while I'm forced to listen to my girlfriends shred me apart." I push my hands against his chest and shove him. Let my hatred overwhelm my fear. "You think I'm going to just pick up your stupid phone, wrap it in a fucking bow and give it back to you?"

Fitz jerks his head slightly. "So, where is it? I want it back." He wobbles a bit. I wonder if he's on something.

"I took a hammer to it and pounded it to itty bitty pieces." I stare straight through his eyes and laugh when his jaw clenches. His left eye twitches. The back of his hand swings so fast, I don't have a chance to react. It lashes against my cheek. My head sways toward the wall, landing against a winter coat. Fitz grabs me by the neck and slams my back into the counter.

"You shouldn't have done that, Lana. You're going to pay for what you did. Dumping me for Stu. Like I'm not good enough for you. Forcing me to settle for Alysa, instead."

I knee him between the legs. He groans in pain. Reaching for the door knob, I grab it and turn. But my head jerks backward as he pulls me by my ponytail then tightens both hands around my neck.

"How tight do you like it?" He asks, tightening his fingers around my throat.

"No. Please don't," I try to dig my fingertips beneath his hands.

"You're going to pay."

"No," I whisper. My mind falls away into a hazy place. It dawns on me that Fitz might kill me. I will die here, in my own home, beside my mom's folded underwear. I faintly hear the door open and suddenly I can breathe again. Leaning against the counter, I gasp for air when I realize it's Demit who has entered the room.

"It would be all sorts of awesome to shoot you in the head right now." Demit's cool voice cuts through the room like a blade. His arms are outstretched holding a gun in his hands, aimed at Fitz's face.

"Whoa." Fitz raises his hands. I wrap my arms over my chest and move to a corner, dropping onto the floor to catch my breath.

"I wasn't going to hurt her." Fitz says, shrugging with a nervous laugh. "It was just to teach her a lesson."

"Shut your hole, you piece of shit." Demit eyes glow black. His jaw is rigid as steel. "What's your name?"

"You're crazy. Put that thing down, man," Fitz says in a shaky voice.

"That's not your name. I asked what's your name." Demit points the gun at Fitz's chest.

"Fitz," he answers.

"Okay, Fitz. You're going to repeat after me. If you don't, I will blow a hole through your heart. Do you understand me?"

"You're crazy!" Fitz howls.

"I may be," says Demit, taking one step closer to Fitz. "If I were you, I wouldn't want to find out just how crazy I am."

"Okay, okay," Fitz backs away, his eyes darting from the gun to Demit to me.

"Demis, stop," I gasp.

"Now, repeat after me," Demit continues. "I am sorry, Lana, for treating you with disrespect."

"I am sorry, Lana, for treating you with disrespect." Fitz says.

"You deserve better than this and I promise to never treat you with such utter disregard for your worth again."

Fitz stumbles over the words, but eventually says it.

"Now get the hell out of here. And if I hear that you lay even a fingernail on Lana, I will kill you." Fitz keeps his head low as he skirts around us toward the door that Demit has opened, and runs. Demit shuts the door and sets the gun on the counter.

"You okay?" He asks.

I nod my head, even though my limbs are trembling as I rise from the floor. My brain is still processing what just happened. Between almost getting killed and seeing Demit point a gun, I'm reeling from shock. I grip the counter to steady myself. Find something concrete to hang on to. "How did you know to come?" I finally ask. "And, what the hell is with the gun?"

Demit lifts his cell phone. "Your text worried me. I drove here the second I read it. I'm not sure why I decided to bring the gun. A sixth sense, maybe. I'm glad I did."

"I'm not sure why I decided to bring the gun," I mimic him. "Really? Who brings a gun anywhere? I didn't think anyone even owned a gun!" My voice is rising. I know I should be relieved that he saved me from Fitz, but the vision of him holding the gun has eclipsed all rational thought.

"Do you smell something burning?" Demit asks.

"The pizza!" We run into the kitchen where smoke is rising from the top of the oven door. The smoke alarm squeals until Demit manages to find it and pull it from the ceiling. I take the black pizza out of the oven. "Shoot. I'll have to cook another one before my mom gets here."

"Want me to wait until she comes home?" Demit asks, tossing the black dinner into the garbage. I shake my head.

"No, she'll be home in about ten minutes." I check my phone. Mom has already texted to say she's on her way. "Better that you're not here. And, hello, gun? What's the story? You scared me almost as much as Fitz."

97

"It's my parents' gun. They bought it after somebody broke into our house one night. He got away with a laptop before my dad spooked him and he ran out. But it freaked us out so much that my mom decided to get a gun. We've never used it, though."

"You seemed to have a good handle on it here," I say.

Demit smirks. "I take it out once in a while and just play around with it. There's something about holding a gun that makes you feel invincible. Powerful, you know?"

"Your mom lets you play with it?"

"She thinks it's safely hidden in the basement. She has no idea I have it."

"Oh yeah?" My heart is slowing down again and relief overcoming my horror. "Is it loaded?"

"Of course not."

"Let me hold it." I extend my hand as he softly presses the gun into my palm. I wrap both hands around it and point it at the door, just like they do on TV. He's right. I feel like I own the world. Like I can take control of my life. Force the haters to leave me alone. It would be so easy to pull the trigger. Too easy, in fact. And, that worries me.

"Easy," Demit grabs the gun from me. "You sure you want me to leave?" he asks, stuffing it into the back of his pants.

"Yeah." I'm not in any mood to introduce Mom to Demit right now.

"Okay. Keep the doors locked. Although I really doubt he'll come back after that."

He wraps his arms around me and holds me tight for about a minute. It helps ease my shaking and I wish we could stay like this a while longer. But I hear my mom unlocking the front door, so I push him away and open the side door. Then watch him disappear into the darkness.

Chapter 11

Karma, Old Friend

October 19

Get to the Nothing

Who am I? It's a question that I ask myself a lot these days. I used to think I knew exactly who and what I was. Because I thought I was exactly the same as what everyone around me thought I was. It's easy when the two match. But all this goes down the toilet when the people around you start treating you like you're someone else. So which one am I?

I have to admit that it's tempting to be the person everyone else says I am. They can be pretty convincing. Which would make me a pathetic loser that nobody likes. This is pretty close to how I feel most of the time.

But what if I decide I'm something else all together? What if I could be nothing at all? Start from scratch. A sort of ground zero. Wishful thinking, maybe. But I'm going to try. I'm going to try to not be me. That me that everyone hates. I give up trying to be what I think my BFH's want me to be. That's been the problem. As long as I'm looking for their acceptance, I'm stuck. Powerless.

I'm done caring about what others think of me!

I changed my hair from blonde to pink. I'm not saying it's revolutionary, but it feels like a step in the right direction. I have to remove the old me, one fragment at a time, so that I get to the nothing. Then I can be whatever I want to be from there.

I'm ten minutes late when I arrive at the coffee shop to meet Demit. Turns out he's later. I can't spot him anywhere among the crowded tables. A woman with short grey hair looks at my pink hair and grimaces. Lining up to order a macchiato, I text him.

He still hasn't responded by the time I get my drink and nab a prime corner table just as a pair of women leave with their babies. My headache from this morning has dissolved, thanks to two extra-strength painkillers. Mom wasn't in any better shape when she stumbled into the kitchen this morning, literally. She tripped over her own slippered feet. Mascara smudged under her eyes. By the looks of it, she must have polished off her bottle of wine after I headed to bed. Or, she'd begun drinking at work and I hadn't noticed. That would help explain why she was so cool with my pink hair colour. Was she half in the bag already?

Demit waves as he enters the shop, holding the door open for a girl who is leaving. She's about the same age as us. Maybe a couple years older. Thin, but not particularly pretty. She smiles too sweetly at him and turns to get a second glance as he lets the door go. *Stay away.* That's the first thought that jumps into my head. I shut my eyes and remind myself that we're just friends. He's welcome to have a girlfriend. Sort of. As long as she doesn't interfere with us. I catch Demit's eye and he nods at me as he joins the lineup to the counter. I smile. Actually, no, I decide he can't have a girlfriend. I want him all to myself.

"So, you're feeling okay this morning?" Demit asks as he sits across from me, sliding a plate with a cinnamon scone on it to the middle of the table.

"Yeah," I admit. "Surprisingly, I feel pretty good. Other than the hangover." We've already shared about thirty messages this morning about last night, so I'm hoping he doesn't push for more details about Fitz. I've kept him in the dark about what transpired before the phone smashing. I plan to forever keep those details to myself. With enough time and effort, I'll forget about it, too. After last night, I'm hoping Fitz's days of harassing me are over.

"So, I guess you have your mom all wrong," he says, taking a sip from his cup.

"Pff." I roll my eyes. "I think she came home half-drunk, that's why. When she saw me this morning on my way out the door, she did this big dramatic sigh. Like I'm such a huge disappointment. She even grabbed a chunk of my hair and rubbed it between her fingers like it was some cheap fabric."

"Did she say anything?"

"Yeah. She said it's a good thing that the pink will wash out in a week."

"Isn't it permanent?" Demit asks.

I nod. "Yep. I didn't have the heart to tell her that, though. By the end of the week, she'll be used to it and won't take the news so hard. She asked about you."

Demit's eyebrows lift.

"She wants to meet you. Even though I told her you're not my boyfriend. She doesn't like you hanging around our house without her knowing you. Of course, I didn't mention that you happened to save my life last night and that you're the last person on the planet she needs to worry about."

The truth is, I almost spilled the beans last night. She'd been so relaxed about my hair. But when the conversation moved to school, things went sour instantly. Just one comment about me and Alysa not getting along. And, boom. Rapid-fire questions about my life, like I was on trial for crimes of popularity. It ended the usual way. Big fight. Stomp to the bedroom. Door slam. Dead silence for the rest of the night.

Demit breaks a piece off the scone and tosses it in his mouth. "Whenever you want," he says. His mouth suddenly stops chewing and his jaw goes rigid. I turn to follow his gaze. Alysa and Sarah have just walked in. They huddle in line together, deep in conversation. Alysa blows her nose. Sarah dabs at her eyes.

"Are the ice princesses crying?" asks Demit, leaning close to me.

"I think so." We both watch them give their orders, then pretend we haven't noticed them when Alysa looks our way.

"What's up with them?" Demit asks out of the corner of his mouth. "Shit, here she comes," he whispers.

"Are you kidding me?" I whisper back.

"Lana?" Alysa sidles up beside me. I look up, bracing myself for an insult. Her puffy eyes rest on my pink hair for an uncomfortable pause before she opens her mouth. "Did you hear?"

Demit and I exchange glances and shrug. "Hear what?" I ask.

"Fitz is dead." She rubs her eyes and chokes back a pathetic sob. "Overdose."

I jerk my head at Demit. His face is slack, drained of colour. Certain that my expression is a replica, I slap my jaw closed and blink before turning back to Alysa.

"Fitz is..."

"Dead!" Alysa buries her head in Sarah's shoulder. It all feels a little too dramatic. I half expect her to yell *just joking*. But even she wouldn't fake something this terrible. With a trembling sigh she tells us what she knows.

"It looks like an overdose. You know he did all kinds of shit, right? I mean, doesn't everyone?" She says in a low voice. "But who saw it coming? You didn't, did you, Lana?" Her words lash out like an accusation. I shake my head. Can't find the words to respond. Does she know about last night?

"All I know is it looks like he committed suicide. Alone in his bedroom when it happened. But I hear the cops aren't ruling anything out yet. Apparently, they're considering that it might be foul play." She lifts her hands and twitches the first two fingers, pantomiming quotations around foul play.

"That's terrible," I squeak out. Demit still hasn't said a word. I stare hard at him, willing him to speak. Kick him under the table.

"Foul play, huh?" Demit says, followed by a long slow sip of his drink. "Hmm."

Alysa drops her hands to our table. "Yeah! But who would want to hurt Fitz? He was so sweet." I focus on her silver manicured nails, curling against the wooden table top. Two thick silver rings on one hand. Even Alysa would know Fitz was the opposite of sweet. Why do people feel the need to speak well of someone just because they're dead? I'm not about to turn him into a saint. Fitz was a pig. Dead or alive.

"Anyways." Alysa straightens her back and flips her hair behind her shoulder. "I just thought you should know." She looks down her nose at me. "And, pink, Lana? Pink?"

Leading Sarah through the tables, Alysa exits the coffee shop. My heart is pounding like it's suddenly grown three sizes too large for my rib cage. Mentally, I understand the death of Fitz is horrible. Tragic, really. But in my heart, I feel only relief. And, if I was to be perfectly honest with myself. Pleasure. Like the world is finally tilting in my favour. I try to remove the feeling, but it's there. I can't deny it.

"What a nice coincidence," Demit says, reflecting my thoughts. "Weird, yes. But at least now we know he won't be bothering you again."

"Don't say that!" I whisper, looking around. "Somebody might hear you." Demit purses his lips together and drops his chin onto his clasped hands.

"Not that we did anything wrong," I say, thinking aloud. "But it makes no sense that he'd kill himself. He was angry and freaked out when he left my house, but I would never have guessed that it upset him enough to commit suicide. Makes no sense."

"And this talk about foul play?" Demit slides the plate with a scone on it to me. "Want some?"

I push it back toward him. I can't possibly eat now. "Did you go straight home after you left my house?" I ask.

Demit lifts his eyebrows. "What do you mean by that?"

"Nothing. I just mean, maybe you saw something on your way home?" I'm not sure why I asked him that. I mean, just because we both wanted him dead last night doesn't mean we had anything to do with his death this morning. I try to chase away my memory of Demit's calm demeanour as he held the gun to Fitz's head.

"Listen," Demit lowers his voice. "We both may have wanted him dead, but does that mean I had anything to do with his overdose, or whatever it was? No. You could have just as easily slipped into his room and done who knows what. What did you do after I left?"

"Me? You've got to be kidding." I burst out. The couple beside us turn to stare. I take a deep breath. "Okay, we both admit we aren't broken up over his, you know, passing. It's suicide, I'm sure. Or he took some kind of drug that caused a lethal reaction. I think he was already on something when he attacked me. Anyways, let's call it Karma. If anyone deserved to die, it would be him." I stop talking, ashamed by my irreverence. Give his corpse a chance to cool before I start my happy dance.

"Right." Demit moves his hand across the table and onto mine. "Nobody but us knows about last night. You have to swear it'll stay between us."

I squeeze his hand and nod. "Forever."

***

October 20

Karmic Lessons

I looked up karma today. Wikipedia says it's the spiritual principle of cause and effect where intent and actions of an individual (cause) influence the future of that individual (effect). Good intent and good deed contribute to good karma and future happiness, while bad intent and bad deed contribute to bad karma and future suffering.

I wonder if what has happened today is a result of karma. The karma that happens to people who do bad things. Two posts ago, I told you about the guy who attacked me. Made me feel like a piece of garbage. Well, this morning I found out he's dead. Ya. Dead. I'm still completely shocked. One day he's just fine assaulting girls and threatening them. And the next day? Dead.

Apparently it's a drug overdose. I wonder when, exactly, karma took over. Did he set the wheels in motion to die, all on his own? Was his destiny set the minute he attacked me? Maybe I played a part in his death. Just the smallest part, though. By being the victim. When you think about it, there needs to be a victim for this whole cycle of karma to work. So, that was my role. I was part of karma's plan. And now he's dead. Would I be horrible to admit that I feel relief? Maybe even satisfaction.

Chapter 12

Too Many Questions

I could barely sleep all night, thinking about what lay ahead the first day back at school after Fitz's death. We spend so much of our lives trying to know every detail we can about the people around us. I never thought, for an instant, there might come a time that I wish I could know less. It's barely dawn when I sit up in bed and open my laptop. I've been getting more comments with every blog post. It's fun to read them. I figure this might ease my mind while I wait for the sun to come up.

My latest post already has eight comments. I do a mental cheer. It's gratifying to know that people are interested in what I have to say.

I read the first comment and my heart stops. Sitting arrow straight I read it again. *This can't be happening.*

I'd have killed him if I were you. You sure you didn't when you saw him last night?

ICUGirl

Panicking, I open the administration screen and un-publish the comment. It was posted four hours ago. How many people read it? Although a few comments followed it, not a single one of them reacted to it. But, who is ICUGirl? Is it just a coincidence that a person posts a comment like this after Fitz's death? I shake my head. Nobody knows what happened between me and Fitz, other than Demit. It's a coincidence, that's all. But, just in case, I text Demit. He's probably still asleep. Only insomniacs and fitness freaks are ever up this early.

Crazy comment on the blog. We need to talk!!!!!!!!
R u awake?

I wonder if it's possible that one of the fabbies has found my site and made the connection back to me? I suppose it's possible, but unlikely. But, then again, I've already got over a hundred visitors a day. My stomach grinds as I consider that it might be Alysa. Even if she has discovered my site, she wouldn't know about Fitz's two attacks on me. Unless he told her. I replay last night's events. Maybe someone saw Fitz leave my house. Would that have gotten back to her?

I pace my bedroom, kicking a few pieces of clothing out of the way. Lifting my Paris snow globe, I shake it and watch the white sparkles settle around the Eiffel Tower. The comment is just a weird coincidence. Nobody knows about me, or this site, or Fitz. I need sleep to return some common sense to my head. Switching off my desk light, I climb into bed. Rest my cell phone on my chest, close my eyes, and beg for sleep to take me. In an hour, Demit will text me. And tell me everything is fine. Then my phone dings.

DEMIT: I think ur overreacting
LANA: Really? U don't think somebody has found us out?
DEMIT: IMHO, no. Probably some 38 yo pedo who lives in his moms basement with nothing better to do than stir up shit on teen blogs
LANA: I hope ur right. Do u think Fitz committed suicide?
DEMIT: Who knows? Whatever... I'd want to kill myself, too, if I was as big an asshole as he is. Or was. My bet is he killed himself
LANA: Really? I hope so.
Wait...
that's not what I meant.
I mean I hope he wasn't killed. Ugh. this is all so weird. And wrong.
Fuck.
What did we do?
DEMIT: We can't b sure of anything. Maybe someone killed him maybe someone didn't.   Maybe no one will ever know for sure. Whatever the truth, one thing is 4 sure.
He's dead. And I'm not crying.
U?
LANA: No.
DEMIT: Stop worrying. The guy OD'd. All evidence will point to suicide. Or too much partying. WE did nothing wrong. Remember that. Last we saw him he was alive and well.
LANA: I know. Sorry to be so paranoid

DEMIT: Don't be sorry. You did nothing wrong, remember
LANA: I know. Y do I feel so guilty?
DEMIT: IDK. Relax
LANA: Ok. See you on bus
DEMIT: Maybe. Not feeling so good. Threw up last night
LANA: No!!! Don't do this to me. You have to come to school! I need you!!!!
DEMIT: Ok. I'll try to make it out my door

I should have known the day would only get worse when I found our usual seat on the bus empty. My first day at Sacred Heart as the pink-haired-freak, and with Fitz's death only two days old, I'd been about ready to melt from the stress on my nerves. Where are you? I'd texted him. It wasn't until the bus had pulled into the school driveway that he responded. Sorry. Can't move.

I try to not be so angry with him, but I can't stop myself. It was he who put a gun to Fitz's head. If he hadn't done that, I wouldn't feel so guilty over Fitz's death. And now, he's at home and I'm at school. *Mercy.*

I'd been expecting to have a miserable day, and destiny delivered it. I'm not at all shocked when the secretary announces over the P.A. in social science class that the office would like to see me at the end of the period.

"Did you hear that?" Mrs. Hendricht asks me. "They want to see you after class."

I nod my head. "Yes, ma'am."

It's about Fitz. I know it. Well, I don't really know it. But I'm pretty sure I know it. And, now I have the next twenty minutes of class to ping pong between yes, you're screwed and no, you're not screwed. I try to drown it all out with my latest mantra, courtesy Demit: *We did nothing wrong. We did nothing wrong.* If I say it enough, everyone will believe it. Including me.

Mrs. Hendricht lets me leave a few minutes early to avoid the crowded hallways. She's a stickler for promptness. I'm not so keen on playing the eager beaver. Something in my gut tells me that Fitz will haunt me as much in his afterlife as he did while living.

"Miss Tiller! Thank you for coming," Mrs. Brullo's voice is exceptionally peppy as I step into the office. "I'll let the guidance counsellor know you're here."

Guidance counsellor? I don't remember requesting any counseling. I steal a glance at the office door and am about to scoot out of here, but the secretary is back before I can take more than two steps.

"Miss Tiller!" She announces as her short round body rolls toward me. Behind her is the counsellor. It's Crumbstache. Well, that's not his real name, but it's what everyone calls him on account of his thick brown moustache that is rumoured to be dusted with crumbs every time he's sighted.

"This is Mr. Retroski," says the secretary before returning to her chair behind her desk.

I nod. He lifts his hand. The 'welcome to adulthood, it's time you learned to shake your hand' lesson. His palm is warm. Sweaty. I resist wiping my hand against my kilt when he releases it.

"Hello, Lana. Nice to meet you. You can call me John." His moustache stretches as he smiles. I don't detect any crumbs. He leads me past the front desk and opens the door to an office tucked in a corner at the end of a short corridor. When I step into the room behind him, my heart lurches. A policewoman is sitting in a chair with wheels.

111

She rolls a couple inches on the seat before getting up and extending a hand.

"Thank you for meeting with me, Lana," the officer says. "I'm officer Maloney." She's young. Maybe five or six years older than me. This is good news. I'm hoping the cop shop sent the rookie because it's an open and shut case, like they do on TV. Unless she's one of those genius rookies trying to claw her way to the top and will stop at nothing to turn Fitz's death into her pet project. I'm worried when I noticed the dark red slash across her cheek. There's a badge of badass if ever I saw one.

"Have a seat," she gestures me to sit on the couch across from her chair. Crumbstache sits on the other end.

"Clearly, you've heard the news about Fitz," she says, pursing her lips. "That he died two nights ago."

I swallow, "Yeah, I heard about it on the weekend."

"Of course," she lifts her hands in a surrender. "Social media spreads the news pretty fast these days. I just want to start by saying I'm sorry for your loss. It's always a shock to lose someone you know at such a young age."

Crumbstache leans his face toward me. "I'm here for you if you need to talk."

"Thanks," I say, rubbing one eye. It must look like I'm starting to tear up because they give me a moment.

She straightens her back and presses her finger tips together. "I need to ask you some questions to clear a few things up. You are welcome to call your parents if you want them here with you."

I shake my head. "No," I blurt. "I don't need to call them, I mean. I'm fine."

Maloney leans back against the chair and crosses an ankle over a knee, then pulls a small notepad out of her breast pocket.

"Why don't you tell me about your relationship with Fitz?" she says.

"There's not much to tell. We went out a couple times in the summer. That's about it," I answer.

"Some racy messages sent between the two of you." Maloney reads from her notepad. "I'm wearing nothing right now." She lifts her eyes. "That one's from you." I feel my face redden. Stare at my knees. "Here's one from Fitz to you." She clears her throat. "I'm fantasizing about you..."

"They were just jokes," I cut her off. "I swear." My chest tightens. I'd deleted all those texts ages ago and had completely forgot about them, until now. "It was stupid. I shouldn't have sent them. But, you know, they meant nothing."

Maloney turns to Crumbstache and nods her head. "Can you give us some time alone?"

"Of course," he walks out the door, shutting it behind him.

Her voice grows soft. "Did you know his phone went missing? His mom says it was stolen. He accused you of stealing it. One of his last texts."

I wrap my arms around my stomach to stem the impulse to retch. How did she get his texts? Can the police get data just from a phone number? My mind races to the bathroom stall. I wonder if someone found the smashed phone pieces and handed it to the school office. Would it still have the photo I deleted? Probably. Nothing is ever truly erased in any of these damn devices. Why didn't I just bury it somewhere?

"I'm sorry to dredge all this up for you, but it's my job. To fill in the blanks."

"I heard it was suicide," I say, trying to change the subject.

Maloney scrunches her nose. Sniffs. "Looks that way, but we want to be sure. Usually there's a note. Some kind of sign." She breathes deliberately out her nostrils, flattens her lips together.

My temple pulses as she pauses.

"You were probably the last person to see Fitz alive," she says. I stiffen as she reads from her notepad again. "You little bitch. I know you did it. I want my phone back tonight." She looks at me. "Sound familiar?"

"I didn't have his phone," I say.

"He later texted you, I'm here." She clears her throat. "He was at your house, wasn't he? Come to get the phone you stole from him. Maybe you got into a fight. Maybe he attacked you. Might explain the fresh scratches on his face."

"No." Did I scratch him? I don't remember doing that.

"Did you have anything to do with the text about him and his mom?"

"No. I swear."

"A witness saw him enter your house, so I know you're lying about something." She smirks.

"Well, he did come to my house." My collar feels tight. A witness? Who was spying on my house that night? "But no. I didn't have his phone. I told him that and he left. That's all that happened."

Maloney does the slow nod. Up and down, up and down. Her pupils drilling into mine. "There's something else."

My left eye is spastic with twitching. I hope she can't see it.

"He has a photo of you. It's not a nice picture, if you know what I mean. Were you aware that a naked photo of you was being circulated?" She narrows her eyes.

114

Shifting my gaze downward, I stare at a crumpled ball of yellow paper resting a foot from the wastebasket. Overthrow. Do I tell her the truth? Say that I know all about my photo?

"I know the photo." I meet Maloney's gaze. "My boyfriend took it. Well, ex-boyfriend now." I shrug, like it's no big deal.

"What's his name?" She asks. I blink and turn to look at the ball of paper again. "You can lay charges against him," she continues, leaning forward. "Distributing photos like this is a crime. You can make him pay for this."

"No way." I stare straight at her this time. My parents don't know a thing about my life, and that's how it's going to remain as long I have a say in it.

The officer rests her back against the chair and shakes her head. "I can't do anything to this guy without your help, you know. We can make him pay."

"No thanks." Fitz is dead. That's all the help I need to move on with my life. Put all this viral photo hell behind me.

Then she slaps her notepad shut and stuffs it in her pocket. Stands up and sighs.

"Thank you for your time, Lana. And, be careful about those selfies. You never know where they'll end up. Or when they'll appear. They can ruin a person's life."

Preaching to the converted, I want to say. "Yes, I will," I respond, standing and rubbing my sweaty palms together.

"By the way," she adds, her hand on the door knob. "Do you know if Fitz took study drugs?"

"Study drugs?" Fitz was a year below me, so I'd never been in any of his classes. But he didn't strike me as someone who cared much about academics. If she'd asked about other drugs, I'd know the answer. Not that I would tell her though.

"I don't know."

"Okay, thanks." Maloney opens the door. "Have a nice day."

I step past her.

"Thanks." I wonder why she's asking about study drugs. Did he overdose on ADD meds? Although I've known a few students to pop pills for learning disabilities or to cram for exams, Fitz didn't seem the type.

"We'll be in touch," Maloney calls out as I pass the secretary's desk. I stop for an instant, nod, then walk out into the hallway and almost bump into Alysa.

"Watch it," she says, flipping her hair back.

"Sorry," I mutter. "I didn't see you."

"I couldn't miss you if I tried with that cotton candy hair." She laughs. "Is this the new Lana look? Nice." She draws out the end of the word like a hiss as she opens the door to the office and lets it shut behind her. I watch her through the glass wall as she casually leans her elbow onto the secretary's desk. Flips her hair both ways, then turns to shake hands with Crumbstache. Her fake smile wide. Charmed, he smiles back, then catches me staring. Clearly, she's no longer mourning Fitz's death. I turn away and hurry to my locker. What has Maloney learned about Alysa and Fitz? I pull out my cell and text Demit.

Police here today abt Fitz's death. Just got questioned. Alysa up next. Im freaking out!

I stare at the screen for a full minute awaiting his response. My body twitches like a bundle of live wires. I take some deep breaths. No text pops up, so I conclude he's asleep. I drop the phone back in my cardigan pocket and take a detour to class, stopping at the bathroom stall to take a peek in the tampon disposal. Empty. A cocktail of bleach and fake lemon fills my nostrils. A sure sign the bathrooms were recently cleaned. I step into every stall and peer inside the disposal boxes. All empty. This is a good sign. The custodian threw the phone away with the trash. Unless he got suspicious and handed it to the office. How long would it take for them to uncover the deleted photo? I look in the cracked mirror. The girl with the pink hair looks back at me.

"You did nothing wrong," she tells me. I nod. Well, we both nod. I am the girl in the mirror. Hard though it is to believe. Girl Unformulated.

Chapter 13

Prescription for Disaster

Demit is in pyjamas when he opens the door. Red and blue plaid flannel bottoms and a faded black t-shirt. Hair is rumpled, no toque. Skin like white plastic.

"You're sure you feel better?" I ask, stepping into the front entranceway.

"I haven't puked in six hours," he answers, leading me into the basement where the TV is playing an episode of *Hoarders*. One of my favourite shows to watch when my life is sucking because it reminds me that someone always has it worse. "So, yeah. I feel all sorts of better."

He grabs me a soda and leans against the wall as I tell him about my interview with the cop. When I'm finished, he shrugs.

"I don't think you have anything to worry about. It's not like she's going to think you force-fed the guy drugs. I mean, he's twice your size. What would you do? Tie him up and jam pills down his throat? She's probably filing the case as an overdose and you'll never see her again."

"Easy for you to say. You're not the one being investigated," I retort. His casual demeanor is irritating right now. "What about the witness who saw him enter my house?"

"Unless this so-called witness was inside your house and saw what we did, you have nothing to worry about."

"And the drugs? Why would she ask about the drugs?"

"Maybe he took some Ritalin for kicks. If it was his first time, who knows what the side effects might've been. Most of us start it in small doses when we're too young to know shit all." He stops suddenly. Turns away.

"What do you mean by most of us? Do you take them?" I ask. He rubs his hand over his mouth, then swipes it across the back of his neck and looks up at the ceiling.

"Not anymore. Well, just once in a while. I was diagnosed LD when I was eight and was taking Ritalin for about five years. Once I hit high school, I stopped. I never felt like myself on that shit. But it prevented the teachers from wanting to beat me with rulers."

"So, you're not LD anymore?" I ask. "Not that it matters," I rush to add.

"I don't know." He raises his voice, waving his hand in the air. "When I started high school, I told my parents I'm done with being *identified*. I wanted to just be me. Didn't want a label. I figured I should be able to just be myself. It freaked my mom out so much that she enrolled me in a private school for gifted students. I hated it. Too many weirdos in one place is not healthy. People like us need to be spread out in the world." He laughs. "By grade ten, I was back in public school but not until I agreed to go back on the meds, which I did. At least for a while. My mom got off my case during the split. That's when she started taking her own happy pills. I guess she figured one doped up person per family is enough."

"Wow," I breathe. "So, you're not taking Ritalin anymore?"

"Nah," He flips through TV channels with the remote. "Once in a while I might if I really need to concentrate on something for school. But I haven't done that in ages." He turns the set off, then drops the remote on the table, and looks at me.

"It's not a big deal," he says, hunching his shoulders. "You're looking at me like I'm the freak show guy who can lick his own ear wax."

I blink and shake my head. "I'm sorry." I hadn't realized I was staring.

"Are you worried that I poisoned Fitz with my drug supply? In a stupor of hyperactivity?" He laughs and rolls his eyes. "I could've killed him at your house. Trust me, if I was going to kill him, it would have been then. It took all my self-control to not pull the trigger."

"I thought you said the gun wasn't loaded?"

"Well. Turns out it had one bullet in it."

"Shut up! Are you crazy?" I practically jump off the couch. How can he be so relaxed about this?

Picking up his guitar, Demit settles into the chair across from me and strums it. "Crazy, yeah. I couldn't believe it when I checked at home. I shouldn't have told you. Forget I said anything. It's no big deal. I took the bullet out as soon as I realized it was in there. Hey, nobody got hurt."

I drop my head into my knees. "This is insane."

"You're acting guilty. We did nothing wrong, Lana."

I do feel guilt. That we are sitting in his basement talking about Fitz's death like it's an everyday occurrence.

Death is rare. Death is big. And, murder? I don't even want to think about it. His calm reaction to all of this is causing my own freak-out radar to spike. I can't fight this weird feeling that somehow, we are responsible for his death.

I feel him sit beside me, his thigh against mine. He rubs my back and leans his mouth against my ear. "The worst is over. Fitz is gone. I don't know what he did to hurt you, but it's all past. Let him have the past." I straighten my back and turn to look at him. His eyebrows bend with concern.

"You're free," he says. "It's a gift."

I know in that instant, I need Demit more than I've ever needed anyone in my life. There's no one else I can trust. He's right. It's over. I sink my body into his and let the worries fade to black.

October 21

Take Back Your Power

I'm growing stronger every day. The BFH's have less control over me now that I no longer care about being their friend. Do you get what's happening? I was giving all my power away to them. I'm taking that power back. I was judging myself through their eyes, which is a recipe for misery. The BFH's feel good by making me feel bad. But guess what? Nobody has the power to make you feel bad but yourself. That's why you need to cut out the friends who hold power over you. Easier said than done, I know. But it's worthy of an attempt.

I realize I only need one good friend. One person who likes me for who I am. I'm lucky

I have that. Do you? I suggest you filter through your friends and find that one special person.

Maybe you have more than one! That's awesome. But just one is enough, believe me.

That's not to say I'm all kumbaya about my ex-BFF's. Not sure I'll ever actually get to the whole forgiveness part. I still hate them. I admit it. And I'll say it again. I hate them. I hope to get to a point where I don't hate them anymore. Did you know the opposite of hate isn't love? It's actually apathy. I read that on a website yesterday about how to stop hating people. LOL. Makes sense, right? So, I need to just not give a dang about the BFH's. That's hard. But it's a goal I can work toward. The whole love and forgiveness thing? No way. Not yet. Maybe not ever.

Of course, I can also just wait for more karma to take care of business. But I can't imagine I'd be lucky enough for karma to strike twice. That was a joke by the way. I have a sick sense of humour sometimes.

***

I didn't sleep again. Another night of tossing and turning and squeezing my eyes shut, begging my brain to shut off. Whoever thought of counting sheep is an asshole. I got up to five hundred and four before quitting. There was no progression toward sleep but I sure felt like I was losing my mind. The last time I looked at my alarm clock, it read four thirty. When my alarm went off two hours later, I wanted to cry. Over the past few nights, I have had a total of four hours of sleep. I can barely function at school anymore. I just want to sleep. The upside is that the cop has not returned to do more questioning. And, Alysa has been quieter than usual.

I must be feeling more positive, despite my exhaustion, because I decide today is the day to enter the cafeteria. It's the first time I've ventured in since the photo. I'm not sure what possesses me to do it today. It certainly wasn't planned. One of those what-the-heck-it's-time-to-regain-my-life kinda' things. After grabbing a pop, I walk toward a remote corner, planning to sit alone and quickly eat my sandwich when Alysa nudges me with her shoulder.

"Hey there pinky," she says in that annoying cheery voice she used to use in our happy friend days. It's been awhile since I've heard her talk to me like that. I look at her sideways. Don't bother to smile as I wait for the incoming insult.

"Holy shit," she laughs. "Talk about an evil look. Do you hate me that much?"

I roll my eyes. "What do you want?" I'm surprised by my response, but here's the thing. I'm so done with all of it. Who would have thought a dye job would have so much influence over my thoughts? It seems to have delivered the wakeup call I needed to stop caring about her.

"What did you think of that chick cop? Complete idiot, if you ask me."

My body tenses. "What did you think of her?" I ask, not wanting to say anything that may arouse suspicion on me. And I don't trust the girl for a millisecond. She'd be the first to throw me under the bus if she had the chance.

"She just asked me a bunch of stupid questions about me and Fitz dating," Alysa answers. "They'll never know what really happened to him that night." I feel her eyes boring into the side of my head. My chest is burning. What does she mean by that, I wonder.

"You don't really think he committed suicide, do you?" Alysa grabs my arm. I turn to face her. Feel my skin grow hot and my throat constrict. I try to swallow but can't.

"I don't know," I manage to say, looking at the silver sphere pendant hanging from her neck. I just want her to leave me alone. Walk away and never look my way again.

"But who would hate him enough to want him dead?" Sarah has joined us. She is balancing two bottles of juice and a plate with burger and fries on a tray.

"Well, let's not pretend he was the most loved guy at Sacred Heart," Alysa retorts, then turns to me. "You hated him."

"He was a pig." I say it without thinking and wish I could take the words back the second they're out. I purse my lips. "I gotta go eat," I try to walk away, but she follows me, with Sarah now by her side.

"Alysa," Sarah whines. "Everyone is over there." She jerks her head in the opposite direction.

"Then go over there," Alysa responds coldly. "How desperate are you that you need to sit with the same pathetic people every day."

"I'll talk to you later," I say, hoping to end this awkward conversation and find a quiet spot by myself. I really don't want to resurrect my friendship with either of them.

"Come join us," Alysa offers, with a fake lilt of friendliness in her voice.

"What are you doing?" Sarah whispers violently. "She can't join us! Everyone hates her."

"Why don't you shut up," Alysa whispers back. "Stop acting like a jealous wife and go find a seat on your own. Put on your big girl panties and act like one."

"Guys," I switch my gaze from one to the other. "I'm okay. I kinda' prefer to sit alone, so don't worry about me." There are no two girls I'd less like to be around than you, I want to add.

"All right," Alysa shrugs her shoulders. "We won't force you to have friends. But in times like these, we all need to stick together, you know? I mean, someone in our school is dead. That's, like, a big deal."

I know she's trying to sound genuine, but her voice comes across as cold and robotic. Like she's saying lines for a furniture commercial. Even her frown feels forced. I notice a twitch in her eye that gets worse the longer I stare at her. That's when I finally realize that Alysa has changed. I'm not sure how I didn't notice it before. Maybe it's me that has changed, and I see for what she truly is. Everything about her feels colder, detached. Definitely not someone I want to be around.

"Yeah," I agree. "It is a big deal, but I'm okay. Go hang out with everyone over there. I'm good on my own." I turn my back and walk away, feeling their eyes on me. Judging me. For the first time since the photo went viral, I feel grateful. That I'm not one of them.

It feels good to have the courage to step back into the cafeteria, but I'm already thinking I'll be back to the library tomorrow. There's no drama there. Nobody to interrupt me while I eat, read or sleep. And I miss the quiet. I'd forgotten how loud it gets in here. Or maybe it never bothered me before.

I finish my lunch in solitude and read my novel until I hear the bell ring, signaling it's time to get back to class. Ugh. More Alysa and Sarah time. I'm tempted to skip the rest of the school day. Pretend I'm sick. Go home and sleep. But mom is home all day today, which means she'll barrage me with questions if I get back early. I'm not sure it's worth the trade-off. I'm still debating this as I walk toward my locker when I notice Sarah by my side.

"If you think you're going to be a part of our circle again, just like that, you're kidding yourself," she says.

I laugh. "What makes you think I miss hanging out with you? Trust me. I'd rather die than do that. So you don't have to worry about sharing your precious BFF with me. You get her all to yourself."

"You may think that everyone has forgotten about what a whore you are because of Fitz's death, but they haven't. They're just distracted. Everyone still hates you."

"Thanks for the update. Here I was thinking I might get a day off from your bitchiness. But nope. You can't seem to keep it from surfacing every time you open your mouth."

"You think you're so great with your pink hair and your creepy boyfriend with the tattoo. You're both total freaks and everyone knows it but you. Everyone knows he's a mental case. Why else do you think he meets with Alysa's mom? Because he is a major schizo."

It's one thing to hear her insulting me, but something inside me snaps when she goes after Demit. Creating more rumours and lies. There is no way that Demit is seeing Alysa's mom. She's a psychiatrist. There's no way he would keep that from me, if he was. It's all too much. The hate, the lies, the death, the fucking exhaustion.

My mind turns red with rage and I don't even realize I'm doing it until it's too late. Lifting my backpack to my chest I ram it into her with all my might. She smashes against the lockers, a look of shock on her face. I hear her head hit the metal with a sickening smack. I think I'm going to throw up. A small swarm of students stop to stare at her body slumped to the floor. All I can think is, holy shit, I killed her. Oh my God. I killed Sarah.

A couple students rush to her aid. Shaking her shoulders, calling her name. I just stand there. Looking down at her collapsed body. My thoughts now catching up to my actions.

"What's your problem?" I hear a tall kid with blonde hair yell at me. Crumbstache comes rushing to the scene, calling through the crowd that is assembled around Sarah's body. "Everybody move away. Give her space."

At first, I think he's talking about me, but no. He doesn't know yet how this transpired. That I'm the one responsible. The monster who smashed another girl against the lockers.

"What happened?" he asks the two girls flanking Sarah.

"It was her." They point in my direction. I have yet to move an inch. Like I'm waiting for my punishment. No point in running. "She pushed her for no reason."

When Sarah opens her eyes, I feel a rush of relief. Of course, I didn't kill her. How ridiculous to think I'm capable of that with one silly push.

"You've had a concussion." I hear Crumbstache explaining to Sarah. "We need to get you to the hospital." He looks at me for an instant and scowls.

"I don't know what happened, but we will discuss this tomorrow morning. We're all dealing with a lot of stress right now. Be in the office first thing tomorrow morning to talk."

I nod before stepping backward and walking toward my locker. I didn't mean to do it, I want to explain. *It was all her fault.* Don't you know how much abuse I've taken? Isn't something going to eventually break? I can only hold it together for so long.

But they don't want to hear that kind of bullshit. I'm the clear villain here. And if there ever was going to be sympathy for what I've been through, it's gone now. I grab my things and leave the school. I can't bear to finish out the day, and going home doesn't interest me. Who knows how soon before the school contacts my mom with the news that her daughter almost killed one of her girlfriends. I wonder if I'll be charged with assault. Add this to the list of accusations against me. First Fitz, now Sarah. For the thousandth time since the photo went viral, I ask myself how life got so messed up.

I could run away. Pack some clothes, raid what little money I have in my bank account and move to Toronto. Hide out in some hostel or join the runaways everyone hears about but no one knows. But I'm not sure I can handle a life on the street. I like a comfortable bed. And a hot dinner every night. Frosted flakes in the morning. No, I'm way too soft for the life of a runaway.

The coffee shop is a fifteen-minute walk away, so I decide to head there. It's actually freezing today, and I didn't wear my winter coat. The trek there feels longer than usual as I scrunch my fingers together to keep them from getting too frozen. Thankfully, there's not a Sacred Heart student in sight when I arrive. Sitting with my hot tea, I close my eyes between sips and try to remember the days before I screwed up my life. It was an easier time, for sure, but I wasn't any happier. Not really. I was oblivious. Too wrapped up in my head to notice that my girlfriends actually hated me. And that my boyfriend used me as much as a source for bragging as I did him. Likely telling his buddies about everything I did to please him. While I got to carry the honour of being the girlfriend of the hottest senior in school. A fair trade off, I guess. But, not really. My life had turned to shit long before it became clear to me.

"Hiding out in the coffee shop?" I jerk my head toward the voice and see Alysa. *Oh mercy.* Definitely not the person I want to see right now. Well, ever. I sigh.

"When did you get so bad ass, Lana?" She has a coffee in hand already.

"I don't feel like talking right now," I mutter, staring into my tea. "Shouldn't you be in class?"

"Shouldn't you?" She asks, pulling out the chair across from me and sitting down. "I heard what happened. Sarah's a bitch. I'm sure she deserved it. Remember that time in grade eight when she told everyone we were the ones who had written nasty things about the new girl in the bathroom?"

I shake my head. "Actually it was you that accused me and Sarah of doing it. Remember?"

"Oh whatever. You know what I mean," Alysa flips her hair. "She did that kind of thing all the time." I lift my head to look at her, ready to finally tell her what I think about her. A self-absorbed, lying, two-faced, pathetic excuse for a human being. But something stops me. Her eyes are like sunken beads, surrounded by black circles. I wonder when was the last time she slept a full night. Like me, she appears to be barely holding it together. But I don't know what her excuse is.

"You okay?" I ask. It's more out of curiosity than concern.

"What's that supposed to mean?" she asks. "Do I not look okay?" She looks over her shoulder. "Did you hear something? Like a clanging sound."

I shake my head. "No."

"That..." She twists her head to the left. "Did you hear it? That annoying sound."

I listen to the sounds of a refrigerator door opening and closing behind the counter, the swish of a cappuccino machine and shake my head again. "You sure you're okay?"

"Do I not look okay?" Alysa asks for a second time. "I'm exhausted. Pulled an all-nighter getting a scholarship application done. My parents will kill me if I don't get at least two. Maybe if they didn't force me to take every shit bag science and math course on the planet, my marks would actually be high enough."

I'm pretending to look like I care when I remember that I don't have to pretend anymore. Old habits, and all that stuff. Yawning, I hope she gets the hint that I'm done talking to her. She's always done well in school, so there's no sympathy from me.

"I really should sleep, but I have to cram for a test tomorrow." Lifting her bag onto her lap, she unzips it and pulls out a small orange container with a white lid. "Want any?" she asks, flipping the lid off and taking two white pills out.

"Are you joking?" I scowl. She shrugs, then tosses both pills into her mouth before guzzling her coffee and smacking the cup down on the table. Punching the centre of her chest with her fist, she coughs a few times. "Damn, I hate it when they get stuck."

"What are they for? Are you sick?"

"It's just my brother's meds. You know he has ADD. I have to pull another late night tonight. Fuck. When am I going to stop procrastinating? Thank God for these darling little pills. They are saving my life."

I remember Sarah's claim about Demit visiting Alysa's mom and my stomach curls. Does she prescribe him the same meds that Alysa's stealing from her brother? Did Alysa give Fitz the pills the night he died? My head is spinning. I don't want to think about any of this. I have enough of my own issues to deal with.

"That's probably not a great idea," I say lamely. I'm about to tell her she's smart enough to do well without help from stupid pills, but can't bring myself to say anything nice. Dropping my gaze to my tea, I purse my lips. There are a few other questions at the tip of my tongue. Like whether she left a comment on my blog as ICUGirl. But I'm too tired and stressed to ask them, much less hear the answers.

"I gotta go," Alysa says with a sigh. "Let me know if you ever want to try a couple of pills. You'd be amazed at how kickass they are. I swear, they'll change your life. I'm sure your marks could use a little boost. Are you even applying to university?"

I shift my eyes up to meet her face. "I'm good." I respond, shaking my head and doing my best to indicate disgust.

"Fuck. don't be so judge-y," she rolls her eyes. "Why do you think Demit is such a brainiac? He's on the same damn meds." My chest tightens. How on earth would she know that? Unless Sarah was right. He's being treated by her mom and somehow word got out about it. The thought sickens me.

"Pardon?" I ask, playing stupid.

"Oh shit," Alysa bits her lower lip. "You didn't know, did you? Forget I said anything. I shouldn't be talking about this stuff anyways."

"No, you shouldn't," I respond coldly.

"What else don't you know about him, Lana?" She cocks her head to the side. "Hmm?" I simply stare at her. Can't think of any kind of response. I'm about to tell her to go to hell when she turns around and walks off. Instead, I take a few deep breaths and try to wave off her words like they're pesky flies buzzing inside my head. No business there other than to irritate me. But I know the seed of doubt has already been planted. How well do I really know Demit?

Chapter 14

Best Friends Forever

I wish I'd stayed in my pyjamas. I wasn't even fifteen minutes into the school day when the vice-principal calls me to her office to inform me I've been suspended for one day, effective immediately. The good news is that Sarah is going to be fine. She needs to hang out in a dark room for a few days to treat the concussion, is all. I guess it's also good to know that, apparently, she's not going to charge me with assault.

I didn't earn any brownie points when I laughed at that. The vice-principal had asked me what I found so funny.

"You have no idea," was all I could muster. When she pried me to share more details, I said nothing. It would take at least an hour to list all the ways she and Alysa have abused me. But, all I want more than anything is to put this behind me. Get through the school year and never see or speak to anyone related to this school again. Except

Demit. But I'm even wondering about him, now. How well do I really know him?

It was a long walk home. Although the vice-principal had advised my mom to pick me up when she shared the good news over the speaker phone, she said she couldn't leave work any time soon. I was relieved. All I want to do is go back to bed. Last night was as restless as the one before it and my eyes can barely stay open by the time I walk in the front door. But, lucky me. Mom is home, after all.

She's still in her housecoat, nursing a cup of coffee, as she walks across the hallway to greet me with a scowl. I don't have to wonder too hard to figure out where I've picked up my habit of lying.

"Suspended, Lana?" her voice is raised. "You got suspended for giving your friend a concussion? I hope you have a good explanation for this. Well, any explanation."

I drop my bag to the left of the entranceway and kick off my shoes. "I don't want to talk about it. I'm going back to bed."

"I don't give a rat's tail if you don't feel up to talking about it. We need to discuss this right now." I'm already halfway up the stairs by the end of her sentence.

"Come down here right now young lady. You are not walking away from this conversation!" I stop, resting my fingers on the handrail.

"Okay," I relent, backtracking my steps until I'm facing her. She motions me to the kitchen where she sits at the table and points to the chair opposite her.

"What's going on?" she asks after taking a sip of her coffee.

"It's not what you think," I'm quickly developing a story in my mind, kicking myself for not working on it during the walk home. "I literally fell into her and she smashed into the lockers."

"What does that mean, you fell into her."

"It means she wasn't paying attention as I was walking backwards. Stu was tossing me his bag, and I kinda' was running backwards to catch it. Then suddenly Sarah is right behind me and, I guess the way she was standing, lost her balance when I smashed into her. And she fell."

Mom stares at me, unflinching. I can't tell if she knows I'm full of shit, or not. More than likely she's trying to determine if she's going to pretend to believe me, or not.

"That sounds ridiculous," she finally responds. "Why didn't you explain this to the vice-principal then?"

"What would be the point? She's going to believe what she wants to believe. Other kids say they saw me push her. They're all lying and she just needs to find someone to punish. So, I'm not going to fight it."

"Well, you should fight it. Now you have a suspension on your record." I roll my eyes.

"So what? I'm done after this year anyways. And it's just one day. There's nothing we can do to fight it. Just leave it and everything will be back to normal soon enough. I need a break from that fucking school anyways."

"Watch the language, Lana." Mom folds her arms across her chest and breathes in deeply as her eyes wander to the window at her left. "Your father is not going to be happy about this."

I lift my eyebrows. "Can I go to my room now?" I ask, pushing the chair from the table. She nods before dropping her forehead into her hands.

"Why do I get the feeling you're hiding a lot from me these days?" She asks. I stop briefly at the kitchen doorway. She's more perceptive than I would have expected.

"I don't know why you feel that way these days, Mom. I've always hidden a lot from you." I leave the kitchen, hearing my mom exhale loudly. I know that line will make her cry. I don't even care. When I land on my bed, sleep comes almost immediately.

October 25

Karma Made Me Do It

I got a wild theory, so hear me out. What if I was the channel for karma? You know how sometimes you hear about a person who everyone knows is not a good person gets hurt, or something? And you say, well, maybe it's karma. He had it coming. Now imagine if the bad thing that happened was because another person did it to them. Like the person got robbed. We still say it's karma, even if it was delivered by a person and not just some random act of nature, like being struck by a major illness.

Here's where my theory gets a bit whack. So, let's say a certain BFH is being super nasty to me (like, what else is new). If, in the process of her being nasty, a random act happened that caused her harm (like she tripped and broke her nose), then we can all agree that it was karma and she deserved it.

Now let me put all this into context. Today, BFH was being her super witch self to me for no reason at all. I snapped and pushed her into a locker. I am not a violent person,

---

but it was liked I blacked out and next thing I know she's collapsed on the floor and has a concussion. In a way, she deserved it. And, in a way, I delivered the karma that was coming to her. I was the CHANNEL for karma to do its job.

I told you my theory was whack. My school doesn't agree with it though... I've been suspended for a day. But here's the truth. I don't feel bad. She has had it coming for a long time. I'm not willing to put up with the abuse anymore.

I have the power to stand up for myself. I'm going to use it.

***

I'm starting to watch my third movie of the day when I hear Mom open the front door. The sky is dark now. The school day finished a few minutes ago. This whole suspension thing isn't so bad, if you ask me. Although eating a full bag of potato chips probably isn't a good habit to get into. I make a quick promise to myself to stay away from carbs tomorrow.

Between movies, I consider the possibility that Demit is seeing a psychiatrist. More specifically Alysa's mom. I haven't brought myself to ask him yet. Afraid to hear the answer, I guess. He's been gone all day, anyways. Some kind of smarty pants field trip for the school geniuses. They were advised to leave their phones at home to avoid distractions. The last text I sent was just after my suspension was announced. He has yet to respond so I assume he heeded the school's advice.

"Lana!" Mom calls out from the hallway. "It's Alysa!" I almost spew chips from my mouth. What the hell is she doing here? I'm trying to figure out a way to not have to get up and say hello when Alysa walks right into the den where I'm still sprawled across the sofa.

Mom trails her. "Isn't this such a nice surprise? Alysa, you haven't been here in ages! I was beginning to think you and Lana were no longer best friends." I clear my throat, still not moving from the sofa.

"I've just been busy," Alysa answers. "Lana and I will always be best friends, right Lana?" I finally pause the movie and look up.

"Yep, till hell freezes over. How cold is it out there today?" I ask as Alysa glares at me.

"Can I get you something to drink? I'm cutting some fruit, would you like some strawberries and cantaloupe?"

"Mom, we're fine," I skooch my butt up a little so I'm almost sitting upright.

"I'll bring some in," Mom says, ignoring me completely.

Alysa crosses the room and sits at the edge of a chair, drops her elbows to her knees and leans forward. "How was your day off?"

"Fine," I reply coolly. "Why are you here?"

Alysa closes her eyes and draws the palms of her hands together. Takes a deep breath. "I just wanted to see how you're doing. That's what friends do, you know?"

"Oh, I get it." I laugh. "So, now we're friends, are we? Hmmm, I guess I missed that memo."

"Don't be such a bitch." Alysa's tone drops. Her eyes widen as she suddenly leaps from the chair and drops to her knees beside me on the sofa. Her hands in a pleading position. "You don't understand." Her voice drops to a whisper. "I can't go on like this. I need more meds."

I sit up, lowering my feet to the carpet. "What are you talking about? The ADD pills?"

"Yes!" Alysa grabs my knees. "My mom found out I've been taking my brother's pills and she's hidden them all, or thrown them out, what fucking ever. She's cut me off!" Her eyes are wild with desperation. I notice the circles below her eyes are darker than ever. Her hair looks unwashed and her usually flawless skin is reddish around her nose and on her chin.

I rip her hands off of me. "You're a mess, Alysa. Get a frigging grip!" I'm whispering now, too. Not wanting my mom to hear any of this. "What am I supposed to do? Suddenly get diagnosed with some hyperactive disorder?"

She rolls her eyes. "No, stupid. Your boyfriend. Demitri or whatever his name is. He can get me more meds. You need to get his meds for me."

"No way," I stand up and take a few steps away from her. "You need to leave."

"Lana, you don't understand." Her hands grip together at her chest. "I can't sleep. I can't think straight. If I don't get more, I'm going to screw up all my grades and never get into any university, and become a massive failure in life. Drive a shit car, live in my parent's basement, and work as a waitress at some hotel buffet to make ends meet. Is that what you want for me? Your best friend?"

I start laughing. I can't help it. The absurdity of this moment is too much. Besides the fact that this scenario she's painted is just another self-absorbed attempt at getting her way through whatever means possible, I love that she wants me to believe that I play any part in facilitating this fantasy pity fest.

"I actually don't care what happens to you," I admit. "But even if I did, there's no way I can help you get your stupid drugs. And anyways, Demit doesn't take them anymore."

Alysa rises to her feet. "Yeah he does. I see my mom's notes. She wrote him a prescription just last month."

A knot forms in my chest. The thought that Alysa knows any part of Demit's personal life is hard to take. "You're a liar."

"I'm the liar?" She half laughs, half coughs. "Demit's the liar. How much do you really know about him? Hmmm?"

"Get the hell out of my house."

"Mrs. Tiller?" Alysa walks past me and toward the kitchen. "Did you say you had some fruit? I'm actually kinda hungry." My fingers are practically trembling from the urge to strangle her.

"Of course! Come on in," my mom responds. "Right on the counter. Help yourself."

I follow Alysa into the kitchen. "Alysa was just saying she has an appointment to get to, so unfortunately, she's got to get going."

"It's fine," she says, shrugging.

"No, really," I stand at the doorway. "We shouldn't keep you. Let me walk you out." I move toward the doorway and wait for Alysa to finally follow me. Surprisingly, she leaves the kitchen.

"I've made your life a living hell before," Alysa seethes. "I can do it again."

"Is that right? Now you're threatening me?" I shake my head. "Get your fat sorry ass out of here and don't ever talk to me again."

"My ass is not fat," she looks at me through slit eyes. "And you ain't seen nothing yet, Girl Unformulated." My entire body freezes at her words.

"You know?"

"Hell ya," she smiles, opening the door. "See you tomorrow. Make sure you got what I need."

I follow her out. "So what if you know? I'm not doing anything wrong with my blog."

"I'm not sure the cops know yet, do they?" Alysa asks. "I told you they were stupid. Be thankful that they're so useless. And that nobody knows about your secret little blog where you write about all the students you hate at Sacred Heart." She walks to her car and opens the door. "Ain't karma a fucking bitch?"

My mind is racing as I step back into my house. I hear my mom talking to me, but nothing is registering. Grabbing my phone from the sofa, I head upstairs and shut myself in my bedroom. I feel drained of energy except for the deafening throb between my ears. A gazillion questions are jumping in and out of my mind. What does she know? What would happen if the cops found my blog? Did she write the comment about Fitz? Would she actually tell the police? Would I be considered a suspect again in Fitz's death? I'm going to puke. But first, I need to text Demit. As if he hears my thoughts, I get a text from him that second.

DEMIT: *You're suspended? Damn. That sucks. You feeling ok?*
LANA: *Hell. No. Alysa knows I'm girl unformulated. She is out of control and I am so so so so so screwed. I need to see you asap*
DEMIT: *It's ok if she knows. It was bound to happen. You've done nothing wrong. I can meet you in two hours at the park down street from your house. K?*
LANA: *Two hours??? And what do you mean it was bound to happen? You never told me people from school would find my blog. Why didn't you warn me?*

DEMIT: Take a deep breath. I know this sucks. But you must have known people would find your site. It's the internet! That's how it works. You've done nothing wrong. Why do you keep acting like you're guilty? Stop. Please.

I shove the phone in my pocket. I can't deal with this. Of course, I knew it was possible that the fabbies might eventually find my site. I just never really considered how or when it would happen. And, how I would feel about it. I feel exposed. The blog was helping to liberate me, and now that familiar feeling of imprisonment is coming back. Like Alysa has cornered me. Again.

I text Demit, begging him to meet me sooner. He relents. We are meeting in an hour. It's still too long a wait, but I guess I have no choice. I respond okay, then sit on my bed and wait, wondering how I'm going to get his meds.

Chapter 15

A Late Night Visit

It's late. When I announced I'd be stepping out around ten to meet friends, Dad said, in no uncertain terms, would I be allowed out given my suspension. His words, not mine. Ironically, after begging Demit to meet me in an hour, I found myself unable to leave the house. Dad had come home early, mad as hell at me. And, I'd been instructed to stay on the main floor all night. Forced family time as punishment, I guess.

Thirty minutes ago, they finally went to bed. Well, Dad is passed out on the couch with the TV on and Mom is in bed. I haven't snuck out my window in a while. So, it actually feels kinda fun to be doing it again. A bit of the old Lana back. Rebellious-gotta-see-my-guy Lana. Turns out there are some good parts of the old me that might be worth keeping.

Carefully, I close the window behind me and crawl to the corner of the roof just above the living room window, being careful not to drop the bag I'm holding. It's a second-storey jump, so the only way to land safely is to lower myself over the ledge until I'm hanging by my fingers. I let go, and land in the juniper bush, falling over as I usually do.

"Nice work!"

I almost leap out of my own skin. "Shit!" Stepping out of the bush, I wipe myself off. "Demit, you scared me!"

He laughs. "I should have filmed that. Obviously, it wasn't your first time."

I roll my eyes. "No, not my first." As we start walking, I open the bag and pull out of bottle of gin.

"Whoa, what's that for?" Demit asks.

"A little Friday night entertainment, that's what it's for. I've had a crappy couple of days, and that's putting it super mildly." Unscrewing the lid, I take a swig out of the bottle. It burns my throat as it goes down. I hand it to Demit.

He does the same. After another gulp, I put the bottle back in the bag. We end up turning into the park off my street. I sit on a swing and he takes the one next to me. The air is cool, our breath comes out as wisps of smoke. There are no lights surrounding us, it feels like we're the only ones awake in this sleepy neighbourhood. If we don't count the squirrel scrambling across the ground.

I run through what happened with Alysa, feeling my blood pressure rise with each passing minute, pretty much out of breath by the time I've finished telling the story. I'm careful to leave out the part about the medication. Not sure how I will broach that subject yet.

"So she came to threaten you?" Demit asks, his swing slowing down. "But why? I don't get it. What is the point?"

Of course he's not buying my story. I'm bursting to ask him about his ADD and whether he visits Alysa's mom for treatment. But dreading it just as much. Dragging my feet against the graveled ground, I slow my swing until it comes to a complete halt. He stops, too. We stare at one another. His face is illuminated by the moon overhead. I notice the contours of his face, the high cheekbones that I'd never paid any attention to before now, and the strong jaw line. He reaches his hand over to touch mine, sending tingles up my arm.

"Is there something you want to ask me?" His voice has an unusual tenderness to it. I wonder if it's possible that I'm actually falling for Demit. And whether I want to put that all at risk by asking him what I need to ask him.

I take a deep breath. "Are you taking ADD meds?"

"What the hell kind of question is that?" Demit asks, his voice dark. "I already told you I don't take them anymore and if I did, why would you care?"

"I'm sorry," I sigh and dip my head back to look at the stars. "It's Alysa. She says you've been seeing her mom for treatments. And that you're getting ADD prescriptions."

"Oh, you're taking her word before mine. That makes a lot of sense."

"No," I try to hang on to Demit's hand but he lets go of mine and rises from the swing. "You don't understand. It's not that I don't believe you. It's complicated. Why is everything so damn complicated?"

"Enlighten me," Demit says, "Come on, let's walk." He extends his hand to me and I take it.

"She's taking these stupid pills for ADD that she gets from her brother." I explain. "She says she needs them to get good grades and to get into university. Now her mom has found out and she's taken all the pills away and Alysa is freaking out. Like really freaking out. She actually looks like hell. I don't know if she sleeps anymore. She's a complete lunatic. The real reason she came to my house today was to tell me to get more meds from you or she'll tell the cops about my blog."

"Just when I thought she couldn't be more crazy," Demit shakes his head.

"So, have you been seeing her mom?"

"Yeah, I had to see her. My mother made me go. Trust me, I would never have gone if I'd known that it was Alysa's mom. But it was too late when I realized that connection. And, yes she gave me a prescription even though I said I don't need anything," Demit explained. "I haven't filled it. I told you, I don't take the meds anymore. I hate how they make me feel. I'm not myself when I take them, which I guess is the point. People prefer me sedated, apparently."

"I don't," I say.

"Does that make you crazier than me or more sane than me?" Demit pulls me to him and wraps his arms around my waist.

"What if it just makes me me, and you you." My heart is blanketed in warmth as I draw myself deeper into his embrace. He lowers his face and softly brushes his lips against mine.

"Hmm, that's nice," he says.

"So nice," I say as I press my mouth against his and our tongues meet. I realize I've been wanting this for a long time, without really knowing until now. It's a long intoxicating kiss that lets me forget that a world exists outside of this moment. I don't want it to end, but my mind allows thoughts of Alysa to creep back in. I guess, Demit has the same problem. He pulls away and sighs.

"So what are we going to do about Alysa?"

"Ugh," I grab his hand and we start walking again. "I don't know." The question is a stark reminder of my disastrous life and I feel the familiar sense of desperation swell inside of me. We continue in silence for a long time, stealing sips of gin every few steps.

"I can fill the prescription and give you the pills," he eventually offers. "Then she's out of your hair for now, at least."

"Then what? We wait until she runs out again and comes asking for more? The school year is only two months in. I don't want to be her little pill bitch for the rest of the year." I don't even realize how fast we've been walking, or where we've been going. But suddenly I realize we are on Stu's street. I must have led the way without thinking. My chest tightens, gripped with hatred for the person who started this mess in the first place.

"Asshole," I mutter under my breath.

"What?" Demit asks, pulling his hand away.

"Not you," I point the house in front of us. "Stu."

"Ah, okay." Demit waits silently at my side while I stare at the dark home. My eyes narrowing in on his window to the left. His back door is almost always unlocked. I would bet my sullied reputation that it's open tonight.

"I'm going in," I announce.

"What?" Demit grips my arm. "Are you crazy? Why?"

"I don't know. I need to see him, or something. Tell him what an asshole he is and how he has destroyed my life." I glance at Demit. "It will only take a few minutes. You wait here, okay?"

"Lana, it's a bad idea. Don't do it. Please. You've been drinking, you're not yourself." I'm already walking away as he pleads. Not sure what I'm going to say, but I feel like this will provide some sort of closure. Or I'll get charged and end up in jail where, it appears, I may go regardless of whether I break into Stu's house or not. I shake the thought out of my head and check the door knob at the back of the house. It turns. My heart jumps. Am I actually going to do this?

I sit on the step and open my bag to pull out the bottle of gin. Unscrew it and take two big gulps. A stern voice in my head tells me to turn around now and go back home. I tell it to shut up and get back on my feet, leaving the empty bottle on the ground.

Opening the door, I stealthily step into the hallway. My head feels a bit dizzy, so I lean against the wall for a few seconds. Chances are high that Stu is home alone. His parents are divorced and his dad spends half his nights at his girlfriend's apartment. At least, that was how things went when I was dating Stu. I still have no plan as I ascend the stairs and eventually find myself standing outside his bedroom door. It's almost one in the morning and for all I know, he may still be out for the night.

I slowly open the door and peer into the dark. Not able to focus yet, I tiptoe into the room toward his bed, until it is clear that he's not here. His bed is empty. I sigh. Is it relief or frustration? Sitting on his bed, I wonder what I actually would have done had he been here. I honestly don't know what I was thinking coming here. My cheeks are heated, and my body warm. I unwind my scarf from my neck and whip it off. Feeling cooler now, my mind grows clearer and I'm suddenly overwhelmed by the need to get the hell out.

As I'm walking down the stairs, I hear the front door unlocking. My heart drops to my feet and I race back to the upstairs landing, and into a spare bedroom. Hold my breath behind the door and peer through the crack.

He's alone, thank goodness. I watch him read a text and laugh, then step through the hallway and enter the kitchen where I hear him open the fridge. This is the best time for me to get out. I take my shoes off and walk down the stairs very slowly. Mercifully, he turns on a video that sounds like a re-run of some late-night TV show. My hand is reaching for the front door when I hear Stu's voice.

"Lana? What the hell are you doing here?"

I catch my breath and very slowly turn to face him. My skin is scorching hot as I race through my mind for some kind of excuse. Any excuse at all to make some sense of his ex-girlfriend standing in his front hallway at one in the morning. The hatred that compelled me to enter in the first place has evaporated. I got nothing now.

"Hi Stu," I respond weakly. "Uh, I, well, I wanted to talk to you."

He walks toward me, a puzzled look on his face. "You wanted to talk to me, so you broke into my house in the middle of the night?" He smirks. "What did you really want?" He reaches out and places his hand on my waist. I have a split second to decide whether I should play along and keep this light so I can make a quick escape, or I return to my original plan and tell him how much I hate his guts and how much he has ruined my life.

"I, uh, wanted to see you again. See if there was still something, um, between us." I don't know if he is buying this. I sound unnatural and wooden. Forcing awkward words out of my mouth, my hand still resting on the door knob.

"We did have a good time, didn't we?" He says into my ear, caressing his hand up my spine and rubbing my left butt cheek with his other hand.

"It was a mistake to come," I say, prying his hands from my body. "A lapse in judgement, Stu."

He grabs my hair and tilts my head back, pressing his mouth against mine. "No, it wasn't a lapse. I miss you, too."

"Stu, no." I pull myself away from him. I can't do this. "Enough. No, I'm not interested. Mercy, man. Get your nasty hands off of me."

Stu laughs. "Damn, you're feistier than ever. I like that."

I glare at him. The game is over. "You are such an idiot. I didn't come here to sleep with you. I came here to tell you to go to hell. To let you know that you ruined my life and it will never be the same. I wanted to take some kind of revenge on you, I had no idea what. I just knew I wanted you to pay for what you've done to me. But I've changed my mind. I don't care anymore. I am actually finally ready to get past this. To not let it define me anymore. I can't even be bothered to hate you. How can I hate someone who I don't even give a rat's ass about? You're pathetic."

Stu appears dumbfounded. His mouth contorted as he tries to make sense of what I'm saying.

"Don't ever touch me again, Stu." I open the door and step outside, slamming the door behind me. My heart is pounding so hard, I feel it in my throat. Within seconds, Demit is at my side.

"What happened? I almost went in there when I saw Stu go inside. Holy crap. He didn't touch you, did he? Everything okay?"

"Oh yeah," I answer. "Everything is awesome." Demit stares silently at me, waiting for me to elaborate. I don't. For a split second I think he saw the whole thing. Peeked in at the front door. But I push the thought away. It's ridiculous. The ache of guilt rises in my chest. I didn't do anything wrong, I remind myself. If he saw anything, it would have been me pushing Stu away.

"Okay, cool," he doesn't press me. "We should get home then." I agree, grab his hand, and lead our way back to my house where I suddenly remember I left my scarf in Stu's bedroom. As panic starts to set in, I remind myself it's no big deal. I can ask him for it tomorrow or the next day. All good. It's a good night for a long sleep.

Chapter 16

The Journal

I wake up with a stomach ache. Something about last night has left me uneasy. I chalk it up to leaving the scarf at Stu's place and try to ignore the gnawing feeling in my gut. Mom and dad are already fighting before I even get out of bed. I turn on some music and cover my head with my pillow and will myself to sleep. It seems to work. Next time I look at my clock, forty-five minutes have passed and the house is silent.

As a result of my suspension, Mom told me I would be spending the day doing chores around the house. Grabbing track pants and a t-shirt from my dresser, I slowly get changed. I have nothing better to do on this cold Saturday morning, so I guess doing housework is not much worse than being bored watching YouTube videos. I look at my phone once more, before heading downstairs, and see a text from Alysa.

ALYSA: *You get the meds from Demit?*
LANA: *No. Not happening*
ALYSA: *You're kidding. You think I'm bluffing? I'm not. If I don't get something by tomorrow morning, expect a house visit from the cops.*
LANA: *Why are you doing this?*
ALYSA: *Just get me my damn pills and we're all good. It's easy.*

I throw my phone onto my unmade bed and swear. No matter how hard I try to put all this miserable stuff behind me, it continues to crop up and send me into another tailspin.

"Leave me alone!" I yell at the phone. Why can't Alysa just let me be. For the thousandth time I wonder what I did in this life to deserve so much misery. I grab the phone and text Demit.

LANA: *Hey, Alysa texted me. wants pills. what do we do?*
DEMIT: *No surprise. We knew she would come after you. Idk what to do*
LANA: *I'm so sick and tired of all this bs. Just want to put it behind us.*
DEMIT: *Let me get the prescription filled. Should take about an hour. You can drop it off this afternoon. K?*
LANA: *Grrr. I hate giving into her. Hate that she always gets her way. I feel like crying. When will she let me go?*
DEMIT: *I know. sucks. She will never let you go if it's up to her. She needs you for her own sense of worth. Pathetic. Want to meet me here in a couple hours? I'll have meds.*

LANA: Ugh. I guess we have no choice. She's not going to give up and I'm terrified that she'll tell cops about my blog. Can we take it down?
DEMIT: Yeah, we can take it down. Is that what you want?
LANA: Idk. I'm getting so much traffic now.
DEMIT: K. Let's wait on that. See you in a bit.
LANA: K.

***

It's a short walk to Demit's house. I'm still feeling off. Like something bad is going to happen. But it may just be that I'm so used to bad things happening that I'm paranoid.

His mother opens the door and smiles. Not a genuinely-glad-to-see you smile. More of a plastic one reserved for polite greetings.

"Hi Lana. Demit just stepped out. He said to tell you to go on up to his room."

"Ok, thanks." I feel awkward taking off my shoes with her at my side. I'm not one for small talk with parents.

"How's the cupcake business?" I ask, itching to run up the stairs.

"It's coming along." She says, crossing her arms. That's when I notice that the house doesn't smell like a bakery. Touchy subject? She waves her arm toward the stairs. "Go on up. He'll be back shortly." I happily oblige.

I've only been to his bedroom a couple times. Both occasions the bed was unmade and his laundry basket overflowing. Something I'd never see in my house. Despite my mom's alcoholic tendencies, she's alarmingly skilled in hiding any hint of family disarray. Keeps everything shiny. I guess it makes a bit of sense, now that I think of it. The lengths she will go to hide her drinking is equally impressive. Weird that I'm just making the connection now. I guess it's one of those things that happen as you get older. One day you realize shit that you didn't realize yesterday.

Demit's bed is perfectly made today. His dresser and shelves uncluttered. I read the title of a textbook on his desk. Introduction to Electrodynamics. I shake my head. Can any two people be more different? Next to it is a music book for guitar filled with Green Day songs. A car slows down outside his window. I look to see if it's Demit. Nope.

Sitting on his bed, I stare at the wall and spin my thumbs. One around the other. His walls are painted a mint green. Apparently, a young boy lived here before they moved in. Neither Demit nor his mom have gotten around to re-painting it, even though a stencil of dinosaurs runs along the upper edge of the walls. I pick up the black book resting beside me and run my fingers over the rough cover. It looks like a notebook. Interested, I open the front cover. Demit's handwriting fills the first page. Thumbing through it, I see that he's written at least fifty pages worth. A journal? Slamming it shut, I toss it back on the bed. Rub my hands and stare up at a red tyrannosaurus. It might be personal, I decide. And, I shouldn't be looking in it.

I stare out the window again and will him to return. I should move the book. Put it in his desk, or something. Reaching over, I grab the journal and rise from the bed. *What if he meant for me to read it?* Sitting back down, I open the cover again. I feel like I did when I first perused a vintage Playboy magazine while babysitting a neighbour's kid. Guilty. Ashamed. Intrigued. And, completely unable to look away. I should not read this. But I have so many questions about him. Maybe if I just read the first page, that wouldn't be so bad.

August 29

Mom says sometimes you do things without understanding why until after it's done. Seems like a backward way of thinking, but in a weird way, I get it. In one sense, it seems like a cop-out for parents to tell us what to do without explaining why. But in the other sense (which is what I think she's getting at) it means we have to trust that the meaning is in the journey. And we won't appreciate the meaning until we've travelled to the end.

This journal is my journey. At least according to my latest shrink. Mom insisted I see one here, too. I begged her to let it be but she worries so much about me. So, I did it for her. To help her sleep better at night. To feel that she's helping me stay on track.

So back to the journal. Doc says it will help me come to terms with my father. Also thinks my brain is so full of shit that it's constipated and needs clearing out. (Not her exact words). But I think she may be onto something. I said I'd oblige. And, I will. Starting tomorrow.

August 30

Today is yesterday's tomorrow, yet here I am with nothing to write. At least, nothing worth writing, but apparently that's okay according to doc. She told me to write as if I'm on Facebook or Twitter or, as she says, whatever you young kids like to post on. I know she thinks that's meant to help me, but she clearly doesn't know me well. That analogy won't help loosen the shit in my brain, so to speak. Aren't those for people who want to expose the "best" version of themselves by updating their status with the "Good News." The Gospel according to thousands of wannabes. Followed by thousands of other wannabes.

In short, I will not be inspired by Facebook or anything else that's online to un-constipate my brain.

August 31

School starts in six days. New school. Zero friends. How excited am I? I asked Mom if I could home school myself. She said no. She's revved up about this enriched program I'm enrolled in. Half my courses are university-level. The other half are just plain enriched. I call it the Segregation of the Nerds stream. Mom doesn't like that. I'm miffed. I won't see a lot of girls (I mean, hot girls) this year since I'll be stuck in one end of the building - with our own lunchroom, and everything! Not that I have any grand plans to date a single one of them, but they're damn nice to look at. Mom doesn't get this sort of thing. At least, she doesn't let on with me around. I've heard her describe me to other moms as a gifted learner. Brilliant. Complicated. And, when she thinks I'm not listening, "A cool nerd." How embarrassing is that. I think she'd rather call me a nerd. Conclusion: she's not utterly clueless about my social circumstances. Note of interest: I did date a hot chick once. Tick that off the list. She ended up being a psychopath, which was very unfortunate.

My little sister starts grade eight. She is not among the gifted elite. At least she worked hard to convince Mom and Dad of that. I know she's brilliant. Well, we all know she is. But, she'll have nothing to do with it. Last year, Mom caught her smoking weed in her bedroom. Sent the family into a tailspin. Like we didn't have enough trouble brewing. I was kinda pleased. It meant she had to see a counsellor, too. It can be lonely being the only head-case-kid in the family. Mom is hopeful that this year will be a fresh start for us all. Because this is Canada! Mom has only maple-flavoured memories of her Canadian childhood where, she claims, everyone is made of good, solid stock.

I hope the year starts off right, too. For Mom's sake. I can tell she's walking a tight rope of insanity (I swear that's a line from a song somewhere.) A single false step and she'll go over the deep end. One committed parent is enough. If she goes, too, our whole family will fall like dominoes.

CNN ticker: American family goes insane among good-hearted Canadians.

September 1

I'd never seen a black squirrel until I moved to Canada. Today I saw one race across the backyard as I was trying to start the lawn mower. It was a very frustrating moment. Pulling that cord that is supposed to start the engine. After a hundred pulls, and a litany of swear words, I gave up and sat down. How hard is it to design a lawn mower that starts with one pull? A worthy invention.

That's when I saw the squirrel. I like to imagine they're the evil cousins of the brown squirrel. Darting around like demons looking to cause all hell in the natural world. Then I watched it pick up an acorn and stick it in its mouth. And I realized they're just simple squirrel folk, except in black. They've got it figured out. Search for nuts. Eat nuts. Sleep.

No complicated thoughts about why they exist. No running around in circles to make life 'easier', to make more effective use of their time, only to find out that they're still running around in circles, except now it's even faster and, damn, when did life get so complicated? Squirrels simply run around in circles. Because it's what they do.

I started thinking about all the technological progress we humans have made over the past ten years. And then I thought about how much more progress we've made if I consider the past thousand years. And I looked at the squirrel again. I swore the little guy was staring back at me. Telling me I've got a long way to go before I get it. He knows what nobody in my species can figure it out. That nothing changes, even when everything changes.

Then I felt depressed. Wanted to find myself a tree and build a big nest and search for nuts and eat until I'm downright stuffed. Live there till the day I die.

But I had to get back to cutting grass. Mom rapped on the window telling me so. I pressed the gas button four times and, lo and behold, it worked. That lifted my spirits.

September 7

First day of school. I kept my head down most the day. Except in class. I'm officially a self-proclaimed nerd. I enjoyed every class and the teachers ain't half-bad. Except for Mr. Moher. His voice is unnaturally high and when he gets excited about a topic (which is rather frequent) he spits. I made the unfortunate decision to sit in the front row and got a spittle shower. Glad I'm wearing my hat all day, but still. Who wants a fifty-three-year-old-man's saliva soaking your hat?

Met a couple okay guys. The girls are okay, too. Geeks, though. All of them. My "kind", I guess. Though maybe not. One of the girls told me I'm "different." I asked what she meant and she shrugged. I think she was blushing, which I'm not a big fan of. Just tell me what you mean, woman! I'm still wondering if it was a compliment. My New York City pedigree?

Bernard is pretty cool. Everyone calls him Beavis. Not sure why, but OK. He showed me three ways to break into a cell phone. All kinds of badass. Then he asked me if I wanted to get stoned after school. Nah. It's not for me. I've hung out with stoners (did I mention I live with one?) They bore me. Tomorrow he promises to show me how to break into the school's computer system. Like I haven't done that before, but what the hell. All in the name of making friends, right?

Then there's this girl. I know... Never start a sentence with 'there's this girl.' You know it's the beginning of heartache when you start a sentence like that. But I did it. So, too late. I don't know her name yet. She's stunning. I caught her eye as we were exiting the school. Me staring like a fool, as I often do. She held my gaze for long enough. Long enough for me to notice she didn't carry that vacant look that pretty girls tend to have. She turned away, but not too hastily. Slow enough for me to see something. A connection? Then she ran into some bozo's car and I lined up for the bus. Let's all say LOSER together now, shall we?

I must find out more about her. Tomorrow cannot come soon enough.

September 13

Her name is Lana. I caught a glimpse of her at the end of the day. Talking to four girls. Well, they were talking. She stood a little away from them. Biting her thumb and looking around for someone or something. After a few minutes, she joined the conversation. A guy showed up, who I assume is her boyfriend. Tall, buff guy with an ugly smile and wooden shoulders. Definitely not the right guy for her. Made my stomach churn to see him grip his arm around her shoulder like he owned her. Said something to her. She nodded. Then he pulled her from the girls and they took off. I tried to keep up with them. See where he was taking her, but the bell had already rung and I had to catch my bus. Stupid bus. At least in NYC, I took the subway. I feel like I'm in grade three here. Actually, everyone seems like they're in grade three, here. Immature. Boring. Coddled. At lunch, the guy beside me (Eric) had an egg salad sandwich with the crust cut off. Really? You're seventeen.

If I told him my dad was in a mental hospital, he'd probably start sucking his thumb and run to mama. I'd guess things like people going insane doesn't happen much around here. Doc has advised me to keep that information to myself. Said it will likely alienate me more. That seems unlikely. How does a person without friends get more alienated? I'm thinking of telling Beavis. Just to see how he'd react. He's the closest to normal I can find here. Sometimes I feel like announcing it to everyone I meet. Just to see the reactions. But it's not fair to Mom. She wants to keep it quiet, too.

Plastic. that's the word I'm looking for. Everyone here is so plastic. I have to meet Lana. She's different. Just not sure she realizes it yet. I have to meet her, (didn't I say that already?) but in a place like this, a nobody doesn't just walk up to a beautiful girl and say 'Hi. I'm in love with you.' Wait. That would seem odd just about anywhere. I need a plan.

I hear the stairs creak outside Demit's bedroom. Slam the book shut and sit, straight as an arrow. Demit's mom pokes her head in.

"You want a drink? A snack?" she asks.

I shake my head, "No thank you." I'm busy reading your son's inner-most thoughts and I'm just fine, I add silently. When she disappears, I look for the page I was on. Skim through the next ten, or so. Mostly small observations of what I was doing when he saw me. It appears I argue a lot. There's a couple spots where he describes me fighting with Stu. Apparently, I lift my hands into the air like two ping pong racquets, too. Who knew? I really should put this down and not read another word. I can't believe his father is crazy. What does he mean by that? So, does that mean he doesn't work in Hollywood? Or is he out of the hospital?

And all this stuff about me. It feels both weird and comforting to know that he was observing me and wanting to meet me long before we actually became friends. I'm not sure if I should be creeped out or flattered.

September 15

The fabbie girls (I've recently learned that's what everyone calls them) were gossiping about Lana today. I stood a couple feet away from the ice queen. Alysa is her name. Tall with long dark hair, never a strand out of place, and a permanent scowl carved on her complexion of ice. I heard the puppet (ice princess' puppy dog follower) say "here comes the slut" loud enough for everyone in the front hall to hear. They shot their heads in my direction and looked past me. As was their habit, they squabbled like rabid chihuahuas whenever she came near. I couldn't hear them perfectly, but the word bitch seemed to punctuate most of their sentences. They've stopped talking to her completely I've noticed, preferring to only talk about her. I still don't know what happened, but it's been almost two weeks since they began making Lana's life a living hell. It's sickening to watch. Particularly how it's affected Lana. She's crumbling like a stale cupcake (I am inundated with cupcakes thanks to my mom.) Hiding behind her long hair. Rushing. Always rushing.

It was a good day for me though. Lana bumped into me. Her bag fell to the floor. I couldn't believe my luck. It was my chance to say hello. Make my move (since a plan had yet to materialize in my head.)

I picked up the bag and handed it to her. She said, "Shit, I'm such an idiot." Ran her fingers through her hair and sighed. Then she looked at me. Really looked at me. And smiled, said thanks. The girls behind me called her some choice names, but I wasn't listening to them. I was trying to drum up the perfect words to say.

Which was next to impossible, since my tongue turned epileptic on me. I could barely breathe, much less introduce myself. Finally, I managed to say, "You're not an idiot" just as her bozo boyfriend yells at her from across the hall to hurry the hell up. And that was it. She flipped her eyes to him, then back at me. I got a quick nod, and she was gone.

I imagine how it would have played out in an alternate universe – if it had divided in my favour. I keep waiting for the many worlds theory to spin my way. A little quantum theory, Demit-style. Somewhere in another universe, this is what played out:

Lana ignores Stu's call, and says "I'm Lana. What's your name?"

I say, "I'm Demit. Nice to meet you."

Then, the universe divides again. Likely, she would have said bye and left with Stu. (Based on the Demit probability which states nothing goes my way.)

In another universe:

I tell her I've loved her since the beginning of time. She:

A) calls me a freak and walks off, never to speak to me again.

B) recommends me to the local psych ward, and never speaks to me again.

OR

I ask her if she wants to grab a coffee one day after school. She:

A) says 'I'd love to.' But I'll have to ask my big football jock boyfriend, first. And I get my ass kicked by said boyfriend.

B) kindly declines, and never speaks to delusional stalker ever again.

Somewhere in the span of time and space, these universes may be playing out. So, when I consider my options. Today's scenario is not so bad.

Speaking of psych ward, Dad was supposed to be released this week but the doctors have decided he's not ready to face the real world yet. Mom cried when she told me. My sister cried. I didn't. I got angry. Why can't he get his shit together? Mom says it's not his fault, but I don't agree. He abandoned us. His mind abandoned us.

Sucks I can't even visit him. Knock his unsteady mind back into balance. Why did she agree to stick him in a hospital in California, anyways? Sometimes I think she wanted as much distance between me and him as possible. I see the look she gives me. I worry her. We're too much alike, me and Dad. He's got his parents, she keeps telling me. They visit him every day. Says he needs them more than he needs us right now. I don't tell her how much that hurts to hear. She has enough on her plate. Which is why I only cry before I go to sleep. Even that – I barely do anymore. In another universe, Dad is out of the hospital and on a plane to Canada. In that universe, our family works again.

September 17

Best day ever. Am I finally experiencing the universe that bends in my favour? I was listening to music on the bus, not paying attention to much when I look up to see Lana standing beside my seat. It was like one of those glorious moments prophets write about in the bible. A light. An epiphany. A knowing. I knew, right in that instant, that our intertwined life was beginning. Of course, she didn't recognize me. Ouch. Really? You didn't get that split second of connectedness when we looked into each other's eyes that one day? Guess it was just me. So, I decided to play it cool. She'd never waste time with a guy who acts love-sick. And, really. That's not my style, as much as my insides are melting with insecurities, I've heard my exterior is generally rock-solid.

I think I was a little too casual, though. We sort of got into an argument when I told her the fabbies were assholes. I thought she'd agree with me? Nope. The assumption here is that she wants back into their fold. I'll have to change that.

Another universe division in my favour – Lana and I both missed the bus home (although she insisted she was waiting for a drive. Regardless, the outcome is unchanged, so it's irrelevant.) The conversation goes more smoothly this time. She looked so sad. Lost. I assume it's over this photo fiasco, which I coincidentally learned today. One of the fuckers at lunch was showing the picture. I secretly exploded a pen over his chemistry assignment. Oops. Blotted it to all hell.

Twists my anger inside-out just thinking about it. I can barely even write about it. If the world unfolded consequence-free, I'd kill Stu for what he did to her. All the suffering he's caused her. Doc says when anger arrives, I can welcome it, acknowledge it, then let it go. I struggle with that last part. It sits quietly inside of me.

***

The door creaks. My head jerks up. Demit stands at the doorway. One hand on the knob, head tipped to the side and scrunched eyebrows. I blink. Stiffen.

"You've read it." He says. His voice cracks.

I nod, shutting the book. "I'm so sorry. I shouldn't have." I hand it back to him, look down. "I should go. I'm so sorry." What I don't say is that I'm also freaked out that he has been carrying all these opinions and thoughts about me. That he's lied to me about his dad. I wonder if I ever really knew him. I stand up to leave.

"Don't be sorry," Demit says. "I wanted you to read it. I left it there for you. I know I've kept a lot from you, but I wasn't ready to tell you." He grabs my hand. "I'm glad you read it. Even though you probably want to run as far away from me as possible."

His hand is warm. "Kinda, yea," I answer. "But not really." I look into his eyes. They're softer than the usual cold gaze I get.

"You're welcome to finish reading it," Demit lifts the journal, removes his hand from mine. I open it, thumbing through the pages I haven't yet read. There are still questions I have, but everyone deserves a few secrets. Don't they?

"No," I hand it back to him. Some questions are probably better left unanswered. At least for now. Despite my confusion, I'm more certain of one thing than ever before. I know he will do anything for me. It's a weird feeling. Like I could jump off a cliff and know he'd catch me. A sort of invincibility, I guess. Maybe this is what love feels like. It's new to me. Comforting. I lean over and kiss him. Push the questions and doubts to the back of my mind. We can talk about them later. What matters most is that Demit is here for me. No matter what. And I need that more than I need anything else in the world.

"Thank you for trusting me with your journal," I say.

"Thank you for not hating me after reading it," he responds, then lifts a small white bag and hands it to me. "And, now, onto our problem with Alysa. I got the prescription. We need to decide what we want to do with it."

Chapter 17

Hug and Make Up

"Oh God, you have no idea how much I love you right now." Alysa takes the bottle from my hand, flips off the lid and sprinkles two pills into her hand.

"Well, I'm glad you're happy," I answer, stepping away from her to return home. She's dressed in tight jeans and heels, so I assume she must have a big night planned. I'm more than happy to keep this meeting short.

"Wait," Alysa says before popping the pills in her mouth and taking a gulp from her water bottle. "I need to talk to you."

I stop and look at her impatiently. Her fake lashes look fresh and black liner coats the outline of her eyes. Even so, she looks like crap. Like she hasn't slept in a hundred years.

"Listen Alysa, I'm done. Don't ask for anything else from me. No more drugs. No more favours. This is it. You can't hold me hostage forever. Just leave me alone, okay?"

"I just want to tell you how much I appreciate this," Alysa purrs, grabbing me by the arm. "Let's do something fun tonight. Like old times. Didn't we get into the best kind of trouble together? Don't tell me you don't miss it."

"I don't miss it." I sound convincing, even to myself. But I know I'm lying. I do miss the fun nights out. My life has been a massive borefest since I lost all my friends. But I hate myself for thinking this way. After everything the fabbies have done to me, I can't even consider hanging out with them again.

"You're so full of shit." She dumps her container of pills back in my purse and wraps her hand around my arm, propelling me in a direction away from my car. "There's a party tonight. You're coming with me. You need a fun night out. Hell, we both do. You can even invite your boyfriend, Demit. He's actually kinda cute for a nerd."

I allow myself to be dragged along, half wanting to let loose like old times. But knowing Alysa is not someone I can trust for even a second.

"I'm not going to a party. I'd rather spend the night pulling leg hairs with a tweezer. Here." I lift the pill container out of my purse. "Have a blast," I hand her the meds.

"Don't you want your scarf back?" she asks.

"My scarf? What do you mean?"

"Stu told me you visited him yesterday. Said you left your scarf and a bottle of gin." She is smirking in a most annoying way.

"Yeah, I left my scarf, so what?" Of course she knows about last night. Alysa has always made everybody's business her business.

"Do you want it back or what? He said it's in his front hallway, ready for you to pick up. He said he didn't want to text you because you were acting kinda weird at his place."

I laugh. "I was acting weird? As in, I told him I didn't have any desire for him anymore and couldn't stand him?"

"That's not what he said." I stare at her through slit eyes. Don't know if she's bullshitting me. I'm starting to wonder if anyone on this planet tells the truth anymore.

"What did he say?" I regret my response the second it's out of my mouth.

"That you wanted him. He told you he was over the two of you but you said you missed him. Want him back. You tried to kiss him." I shake my head in disbelief.

"I don't believe you."

Alysa drops her mouth, eyes widen. "Me? Don't shoot the delivery girl, Lana. I'm just replaying what I heard. I know Stu's an asshole. Maybe he is lying. Wouldn't be the first time, right?"

"I really don't care, to be honest. But I do want my scarf back. I guess I'll go grab it tomorrow."

"I think you should get it tonight," Alysa sighs as if she's pondering something.

"What is it?"

"Well," she drops her head to the side. "He said he was going to throw it out. Said he wants to get you out of his life for once and for all. Whatever."

"You're full of it." This is so ludicrous I can't believe I'm still standing here listening to this.

"But don't worry! I talked him out of it. He said he would hold onto it for tonight, but after that he's getting rid of it." I look up at the black sky. It's a clear night with more stars than usual punctuating the darkness. I focus on a lonely, but bright, one. *What should I do?* I ask. It's my favourite scarf. Mom bought it last winter on sale at a boutique in Toronto. And damn, it's cashmere. I can't leave it at Stu's and risk losing it. *Don't go. It'll be trouble.*

That's what I think I hear. But I want my scarf. I ignore that thought or voice, whatever it is. Probably nothing. Just paranoia. I'll quickly grab it from Stu and go. Fifteen minutes out of my life. Tops.

"Fine. I'll get it right now. But then I'm going home. No party, no nothing. Just grab the scarf and go home."

Alysa parks behind a car a few houses down from Stu's place. In fact, the street is lined with cars and music is streaming from his house.

"You failed to mention that it's Stu who's having the party," I say dryly to Alysa.

"Didn't I tell you that? I'm sure I did." She gets out of the car without even glancing at me. She knows she has won this last battle. I'm seething, but remind myself all I need to do is step in the front door and grab the scarf. Then get out of there. Easy peasy.

The door is practically pulsating from the beat of the music. I don't have any idea why we even bothered to ring the doorbell. My stomach is in knots again. After tonight, I hope and pray that I never step foot into this house again.

"Just walk in," I say, not hiding my growing irritation. Alysa opens the door and we are greeted by a couple making out at the bottom of the stairs. I don't recognize them so assume they're from the other high school in town. They stop when we walk in and move to a dark corner.

"So where is it?" I yell over the music to Alysa who is already wandering off. "Alysa!" I yell even louder but it's of no use. Either she's ignoring me or can't hear me. *Mercy.* There are coats hanging on a line of hooks to the left of the door, above a bench with baskets beneath it. I decide to start looking through the coats. As quickly as possible, I look under every coat and jacket to search for my turquoise and grey scarf. When I get through that, I drop to my knees and pull out the first of three baskets, rummaging through it until I know with certainty the scarf isn't there. Do the same for the other two baskets. Nothing.

Quel surprise. More lies. I rest my elbows on the bench and drop my chin into my clasped hands. I'm feeling so frustrated at this moment, I don't know if I should chase her down and strangle her or cut my losses and leave.

"What are you doing?" I turn my head and look up to see Stu staring down at me with a perplexed look.

"Where the hell is my scarf!"

"It's still in my room. You want me to get it?"

"Yeah, like right now."

He shrugs and turns to go upstairs when Tracy stops him and wraps her arms around his neck and kisses him. She pulls him away from the stairs and into the family room where everyone seems to be congregating.

"Are you kidding me?" I yell after Stu. I really do hate all these people. The one positive outcome from all this is that I realize how much happier I am without them in my life. I take the stairs two at a time and head into Stu's bedroom. Scanning the room, I try to find my scarf. At first, I can't see it. But after a few minutes of looking, I finally spot it folded on the floor between his bed and dresser, beneath a textbook. I am so relieved I think I actually smile as I pick it up and wrap it around my neck. I look in the mirror. Can't resist. It's such a beautiful scarf.

"Admiring yourself?" Stu is standing at the doorway. Walking in, he closes it not quite all the way.

"What are you doing?" I ask, looking past his shoulder. "I'm leaving now."

"Lana, I just wanted to say something," he puts his hands in his pockets, his shoulders hunch forward. "About last night."

I don't get the impression he's about to attack me, so I stand quietly and wait.

"About everything. Listen, I'm sorry. I was out of line last night and the photo." He sighs. "I was wrong to share that photo of you with anyone. I, honestly, did not expect it to spread like it did. I only sent it to one person, I swear."

"You know what, Stu?" I cross my arms. "You were always an asshole. I knew it before we started dating. I knew it when we were together. You're too pretty to not be a dick with girls like me throwing ourselves at you. You don't have to work at making a girlfriend happy because there's always a lineup of them waiting for your affection. I was just another one in the lineup. So, I guess, in a way, that's something you have to learn to live with. Being a natural asshole. But I accept your apology. It's all over now. I want to move on."

He rolls his eyes. "Yeah. Me too."

"Consider this a first step in your journey towards becoming a decent guy." I laugh, slap him on the back.

"Friends?" Stu asks, his arms outstretched. I look at him, wonder if he's putting me on. It doesn't seem like it. And even if he is, do I really care? No, I don't.

"Friends." I give him a hug. It feels like a genuine friend hug. He makes no effort to grab any extra parts of my body. As we pull away from each other, I notice Alysa is standing at the doorway with her phone up in the air.

"Did you just take a photo of us?" I ask.

She smiles sweetly. "It was such a nice make-up hug. I thought you guys would like me to send you a copy."

"What's your problem?" I ask, stepping toward her. "Delete the damn photo."

She pops her eyes wide with feigned innocence. "What are you talking about? It's just a photo. God, you're so paranoid."

"Delete the photo, Alysa." Stu adds. "Lana has been through enough. Just let her be, would you?"

"Fuck off Stu." Alysa shoots the words out like venom.

"You're a bitch, Alysa," Stu starts. "It was you more than anyone who made sure everyone saw Lana's photo. I'm not stupid. I heard how you talked about your supposed best friend every chance you got. Calling her names. Making sure everyone hated her as much as you did. It was probably you who sent the photo to everyone in school. Wasn't it?"

Alysa lifts her palm to her chest and lets out a breath of disbelief. "I can't believe you're trying to put that all on me!" She turns to look at me. "Wasn't I the first one to start talking to you again? To invite you back into the fabbies?"

I'm not surprised by Stu's accusations. Certainly, I've had my suspicions that she was the ring leader. But it continues to sting, no matter how many times it's thrown in my face.

"I don't care." I say quietly. "I don't care about you or Stu or Sarah or Tracy or anyone else. I just want out." I grab the container of pills from my purse, open the lid and whip the contents at her face. The pills scatter across the room and hallway.

"Bitch!" Alysa drops the floor, scrambling to find them. I step over her hunched back, stomp down the stairs, and open the front door.

"You will be sorry," Alysa yells from the top of the stairs. I look up at her. She's dressed in all black. Her hair tied back tightly. For a second, she looks like a witch. A shiver runs down my spine. Then I turn and slam the door behind me.

Chapter 18

Just Keep on Walking

My throat is scratchy as I walk home. I wouldn't be surprised if I was coming down with a cold. Don't know how much longer I can handle all this drama and stress. My heart is beating wildly and I'm trying to catch a full inhale as I cross the street. My breath can't seem to travel beyond the centre of my chest. It gets stuck there, as if hitting a trap door, bouncing back up my throat without having a chance to settle anywhere in my body. I try to slow the breaths down, but it's not helping.

I just need to drop into my bed and sleep. For days. Even better, sleep until the school year is over. Let this misery bypass me so that when I wake up I can start fresh. Demit has texted me about ten times in the past hour asking how the pill meeting went. I can't even begin to explain the crap that went down in a text.

As a car slows beside me, I pick up my pace. My heart pounding. Just what I need. An abduction.

"Lana." I hear Demit's familiar voice and I am finally able to inhale a deep sigh of relief. "Get in. What are you doing by yourself this late?" I walk around to the other side of the car and climb in.

"It is such a relief to see you," I lean over to hug him and plant a kiss on his mouth. "What a night." Demit starts driving.

"You didn't answer my texts," he says. I ignore the slight accusatory tone in his voice.

"Sorry. I had too much to tell you to fit in a text. The night did not go as planned, I can assure you."

"I guess not. I don't remember us discussing a stop at Stu's house." I let silence fill the car. Wondering if he is accusing me of something. And how does he know I was at Stu's?

"No, it wasn't part of the plan. And I didn't want to go, but Alysa kind of forced me into it. I needed to get my scarf, and..." I stop, fold my arms over my chest.

"Why should I explain myself to you. Am I on trial here? Do you actually think I want to spend time with those assholes? How do you know, anyways? Are you following me?"

"I got a photo sent to me from Alysa. Of you and Stu with your arms around each other."

I roll my eyes. "So I am on trial. Now I have to explain myself to you, too. Like I don't have enough enemies in my life. Like I'm not already so alone, just trying to keep my head above water. Trying to not be thrown in jail. Trying to juggle Alysa's psychotic demands. Now I have to explain my motives to you? Stop the car."

"Lana, please. I was only asking a question." Demit reaches over to grab my hand but I pull it away.

"Please let me out of the car." I put my hand on the door handle and start to open it.

"Are you crazy, wait!" Demit grinds the car to a stop. "Please don't leave. Let me at least drive you home. I'm sorry, okay?"

I open the car door and get out. "I am so tired of everything. I need at least one person I can count on. Who completely trusts me and is there for me. I thought that was you." I shut the door and cross the road to the sidewalk to finish my walk home. It's only a couple minutes away.

Demit rolls down the passenger window to try talking to me, but I don't hear what he's saying. Shut him out completely. His car falls behind me and finally drives off after I walk up my driveway.

October 27

Follow Your Gut and Keep Walking

Ever notice the more you try to do the right thing, the more life screws with you? It makes no sense, believe me. And perhaps it's just my own messed up life. Sometimes I wonder if I'm in upside down world here. Where not a single thing makes sense. And every time I try to flip it back to upside up, things get worse.

I guess it goes to show that I don't know what upside up is. Maybe I'm living in upside up already and just can't accept that this is the way my life is supposed to be. Whether I like it or not. Is the key to being happy giving in to whatever life throws at me and move

---

with the flow? Damn, that's a tough pill to swallow. But don't get me talking about pills.

My latest drama is all because of pills. I get the desire to escape. Run away from the pressures and stresses of living. Smoke a joint, get loaded one night on your parents' most neglected bottle of alcohol. Trust me, I've been there. But taking pills every day to be someone other than who you are meant to be? No, it doesn't make sense. As much as I want a break from my circumstances, I have no interest in changing who I am.

I've been blackmailed into supplying pills to one of the BFHs. And, yes, you know who you are... I'm sure you're reading this. She's addicted to ADD meds to get better grades. As much as I dislike this girl, it kills me that someone like her who is already so smart needs to rely on pills to be even smarter. I won't even get into how I've become the supplier because it's so convoluted that it'll make your head spin.

Life keeps getting messier. I try to claw my way out of this hole but it's like someone is shoveling dirt to make sure I'm buried before I get to the surface. The thing is this. Deep down, I feel like I'll be okay. I will survive this. I have to keep moving, that's all. It's like one of those crazy windy, rainy days where you're caught outside and your umbrella gets flipped the wrong way, and you're walking against the rain and wind, pushing to get to that warm dry place. Have you ever NOT gotten there? No. You always eventually get to the destination. You always reach the warm dry place. I guess that's what I'm counting on. Reaching the warm dry place. I can almost picture it. My umbrella has blown away. I'm soaked. There's lightning overhead. And it's so dark I don't even know if I'm going in the right direction. But my gut is leading me somewhere. So I'm going to trust my gut. Know that it's right. To be honest... Do I have any other choice?

So, if you're in a similar situation. Your friends hate you. You're alone. You want to DIE. Hang on, ok? We're all gonna get where we need to go. Just keep frigging walking.

***

A canker has bloomed. Every time I move my mouth, it feels like a needle is pushing into my gums. Add a scratchy sore throat and I decide that I'm not getting out of bed today. I roll over, throw my pillow over my head and fall back asleep.

When I wake up again, Mom is hovering over me.

"Lana? You awake?"

"Yeah," I scrape out. "What time is it?"

"Around noon. Are you sick?"

I nod, sitting up and leaning against my bed's backboard. Mom's in yoga clothes, still sweaty from her trip to the gym.

"It's already twelve o'clock?" I say. Demit must have texted me a hundred times by now. "Pass me my phone?" Mom finds it on my desk and hands it over.

"You feel hot," she says after resting her hand on my forehead.

"I feel horrible," I admit, waiting for her to leave so I can read my texts in private. "Can you pass my laptop, too?" Mom sits at the side of my bed and looks at me. Her lips are pressed together, hands folded neatly in front of her.

"How's school these days?" She asks. I close my eyes and let my head roll from one shoulder to the next. Now? She's choosing now to chit-chat about my life? I feel like a cat is clawing my throat and she wants to talk?

"Mom, it's fine."

"Because you seem to be really, I don't know, absent at home. You're always up in your room, staring at your phone, or just ignoring me and your father."

"Well, I'm sorry if you think I'm ignoring you."

"No," Mom straightens her arms and back. Turns her head slightly and looks upward. "I don't think you're ignoring us. I know you're busy. And, that's all good. I just wonder if sometimes, maybe, we should talk more about what's going on. I mean, I don't know what is going on in your life. At least I used to see your friends. And Stu used to be here a lot. But now. Nothing. Is it us?"

"No, Mom. It's not you." I sigh. I want to tell her it has absolutely nothing to do with her. Nobody cares about her. Nobody cares about me. "Everything is just fine. I'm busy, you know?"

"Are you dating that other boy?" she asks. "What's his name?"

"Demit," I answer quickly.

181

"Yes, we're together. But it's... complicated." I want to push her off my bed. Tell her to leave me alone like she does the other ninety-nine per cent of the year. *I don't need you anymore.* The thought materializes out of nowhere. It takes me by surprise. It's a sad thought.

"Well, are you together or aren't you together? There's nothing complicated about that."

"Yes, we're together." I admit. "I guess." I'm too tired and sick to say anything else.

When Mom leaves the room, I hit the home button and watch my screen light up. Demit has sent about a dozen texts. Mostly apologies.

I'm not sure if I should respond to him yet. Although my frustration from last night has subsided, I'm still hurt that he was so accusatory toward me. He's certainly got a lot of nerve to accuse me of any dishonesty considering that he's been stalking me since the beginning of the school year. And then there's the whole issue with his father. I'm still unclear on that. Is he in a mental institution or what? Lies and half-truths.

Then again, he left his personal journal out for me to read. So, in a way, I guess he made up for all his secrets. I tuck my phone under my pillow. Not ready to deal with all that right now.

Alysa has sent me a bunch of texts, too. I reluctantly review them.

ALYSA: I managed to pick up the mess. All good! Thanks for getting them.
ALYSA: You missed a great party! Why did you run out so quickly? Fun was just getting started.
ALYSA: Damn. Just counted my supply and I'm already low. I guess dipped a little too much into it last night. I need more. Call Demit.

ALYSA: Helloooo! Where are u? Do I need to come for another visit? Text me asap. Seriously.

I'm not sure how to answer her texts. I feel like calling her up and screaming at her. Telling her to leave me the hell alone. But that's just stupid. I'm sure I made it clear yesterday that she would not receive any more pills from Demit. I hate to admit it, but Alysa scares me a little. She has almost single-handedly ruined my life over the course of a month. What else is she capable of doing?

LANA: I can't get pills. I told you I'm done. Leave me alone.
ALYSA: One more time. I need them. You have to help me!
LANA: Let me see what I can do. Will get back to you.

I have no intention of getting her any extra supply. But I need time to think. To come up with a plan to get Alysa off my back once and for all. At the moment, I have no idea how I will accomplish it. I decide now is as good a time as any to text Demit.

Thanks for apologies. Everything is fine. K? Have a new problem. Alysa wants more pills already. Frig. Not sure what to do. Open to suggestions.

As much as I hate how he treated me last night, there is no one else in the world who can help me with Alysa. No one else who knows what I'm going through. I have no choice but to forgive him. And ask for help.

Chapter 19

Is it so Random?

Monday morning comes way too quickly. Even though I've spent the last twenty-four hours sleeping, I still feel pretty lousy. I reach for my phone, then remember that Mom took it away yesterday afternoon. Said I need to focus on getting better and not what all my friends are up to. I was too sick to argue. Now I'm panicking, wondering what I've missed. How pissed off I've made Alysa by not responding to her. And how many messages Demit has sent that went unanswered.

I am tempted to stay in bed, but I actually want to go to school today. Face the music, as they say. Well, somebody says that.

"Mom!" I yell as I head into the bathroom to shower. "I need my phone."

"Your mother is at the gym," Dad answers from the kitchen downstairs. "She should be back in the next fifteen minutes."

With my head poking out of the bathroom door, I ask, "Do you know where my phone is? I need it, like, now."

"No, I don't know. I haven't seen it. Ask your mother when she gets back."

My heartbeat is picking up its pace. The longer I wait to read my texts, the more I feel my panic rising. Another fifteen minutes feels like an eternity.

Mom doesn't get back home until I'm walking out the door. I am beside myself. How does she expect me to survive without my phone? And, go figure, when she finally hands it to me, it's dead. I was ready to lay into her, but she got so bent out of shape looking for the paring knife to cut up fruit for her smoothie that I couldn't be bothered. Mom and Dad got into it, instead, blaming one another for the knife that neither of them have been able to find for the past couple days.

I'm so grateful when I finally see Demit on the bus, I completely forget that he still thinks I'm mad at him. Flopping in the seat beside him, I take a deep sigh of relief. "I haven't read any texts since yesterday morning. And, can you believe my mom just gave me my phone back and it's dead?"

Demit looks steadily at me, his lips downturned. "You haven't read any texts since yesterday morning?" he repeats.

"No. Why are you looking so intensely at me?"

"Have you looked online at all? At anything? Have you heard anything?"

"You're starting to freak me out now. Are you that ticked that I didn't answer your texts? Seriously, I was upset the other night."

Demit rubs his hands over his face and looks out the window before turning back to me. "So you don't know about Stu?"

My stomach flip flops. "What about Stu?"

"He's in the hospital in critical condition."

"What?" I can't possibly have heard him correctly. I saw Stu only two nights ago and he was perfectly fine. Sure, he was a bit drunk. But not as bad as I'd seen other people.

"Was he in an accident?" I ask.

"Nobody knows what exactly happened. Apparently, his father went into his room yesterday late in the morning and couldn't wake him. Called nine-one-one and he's been in the hospital ever since. Not sure he's woken up yet."

My mind is racing. I left around ten o'clock Saturday night. He was perfectly fine. I feel sick to my stomach. Did he take drugs? Just like Fitz had done? I try not to draw any parallels, but they are forming all on their own.

"How is this happening?" I say, my hands covering my mouth.

"I know. It's freaky. The rumour is that he overdosed."

"Like Fitz." We say it at the same time and stare at each other. The thoughts and visions bombarding my head are overwhelming me now. Did Stu take some of Lana's meds? The meds I supplied to Lana? Was Demit so angry about me seeing Stu that he showed up that night to do something to Stu? Or is this yet another isolated random incident that doesn't relate to any of us? Just like Fitz's death. The conclusion does not sit well with me. Life doesn't happen that randomly. Someone did something that night to intentionally hurt Stu. I know it in my gut. But who? And, if someone caused Stu's overdose, then very likely the same person was responsible for Fitz's death, too. My head is aching more than ever now.

"Someone did something," I say. "This is not a coincidence."

Demit shrugs. "You don't know that."

"Please! First Fitz, now Stu? Are you kidding me?"

"There are bigger coincidences in the world than two dumb jocks dying from too much alcohol and drugs."

"Stu isn't dead," I answer gravely. "And how can you be so callous? This is serious."

"I know that. But they're both assholes, so I'm not going to be too upset about it. And neither should you be."

"I'm not upset," I start, then stop. "Stu said sorry Saturday night. And I believed him. This whole photo thing got way out of control. Stu may be a self-centred egomaniac, but he's not the type to strategize a person's downfall from grace. It was all Alysa's doing. And, even though I don't want to defend Stu, I'm not going to blame him for everything that has happened to me. We were good when I left his house that night. That's why we hugged, actually. We both agreed to put it behind us. So, yeah, I do feel kind of bad. This isn't right."

Demit is looking sideways at me. Nods his head. "That's good. I guess."

"I'm not saying Stu's a saint, okay? But he doesn't deserve to be in the hospital either."

"You're a bigger person than me," Demit says. "I can't forgive him for what he did to you. And I don't feel bad for him, either. He got what he deserved." I look down at my hands resting on my bag. Need something to focus on other than this. Something mundane. Requiring no judgement. No fear. No questions about who Demit really is. Who I am. Who any of us are. Are we all actually monsters on the inside? Spending most of our days unaware of the darkness until suddenly there's a window for it to slither out? Whether it's in an action, a thought, a judgement. Or just simple hatred.

"I definitely hated Stu," I say quietly. "I've hated Alysa. I hated Fitz. But am I happy that Fitz is dead and Stu is fighting for his life?" I don't answer my own question. Demit sits silently beside me. I know my answer is no. I'm not happy. But I do hate. And maybe that's my monster. That I've let the hatred fester. Maybe that's how I've contributed to all the awful things that have been happening. I have no intention of letting go of the hate, though. Don't know if I could, even if I tried.

Demit leans over to kiss me on the lips. Despite my frustration and fear, it feels wonderfully sweet. How could someone who makes me feel so special be a terrible person? I don't know what role, if any, that Demit played in Fitz's death or in Stu's predicament. I want to believe he played no part, other than the one I played. He hated. I pray that's all he did. Have to believe that's all he has done. The bus arrives at school and we say goodbye at the front entrance. I don't get very far before I'm cornered by the principal.

"Lana," His voice breaks into my thoughts. I see him summoning me toward the office. "Please come this way." I nod my head and obediently follow his order, finding myself back in the same office from my last visit.

Officer Maloney is blowing her nose when I walk in. The guidance counsellor isn't here this time.

"Hello again, Lana," she says in a clogged voice. "Excuse the cold. I caught that bug that's been circulating."

"Yeah, me too," I say, wiping my dripping nose with the back of my hand.

"Sit," she says, waving her hand at the chair across from her. This time feels a lot more like an interrogation. I'm wishing Crumbstache was here. Officer Maloney's knees are less than a foot from my own. I wonder if she can hear my heart pounding as well as I can. The notepad comes out. She flips through it before lifting her face to look at me. A rash of red surrounds her nostrils. Kind of grosses me out, so I look at my hands.

"You're pretty busy, aren't you?" she says with a sniff. No pleasantries this time around.

"Pardon?"

"First we find out you're Fitz's girl and now I learn you and Stu were a couple, too. Pretty big coincidence, no? That one is dead and the other's life is hanging by a thread?"

"I had nothing to do with any of this!" I blurt. Then clamp my mouth shut. Easy on the paranoid, I scold myself. Suddenly I remember my blog. How did I not think of it earlier? Demit needs to shut it down now. Is it too late? I wonder. Has Alysa already told the cops? Is that why I'm here right now? I don't even hear what Maloney is saying to me, too consumed by the voices screaming in my head.

"Pardon?" I ask.

"I said I haven't accused you of anything, Lana. I'm just trying to get the facts."

"What are the facts? Is he awake?"

She shakes her head. "There's been no change in his condition. Normally I wouldn't get involved at this point but there's this weird thing." She stops talking and stares hard at me. "He has some markings on his body. They're fresh. Like someone used a knife on him. Carved into his skin."

"What?"

"Why would somebody want to make their mark on Stu? Perhaps for revenge? Get him back for hurting her. Show she's the one who gets the upper hand. I get it. The guy sent out your porno pic to all his friends. I'd be pissed. I'd definitely consider cutting his balls off, or something."

"Are you crazy? No," My head is pounding so hard that I see black spots around the officer. I can barely see straight. "I wasn't mad at him. I mean, I was mad. But we had made up. I put it behind me. I would never do anything like that. I don't understand."

"You know he had a party Saturday night though?"

"Yes, I know."

"You were there?"

I pause before answering. I was barely there. Does twenty minutes count as being there? Then I decide being honest has got to be the best way to go. I have nothing to hide. "Yes, I stayed for about twenty minutes. That's it."

"You're sure about that?"

"Yes, absolutely."

"Did anyone else see you to corroborate this?"

I pause again. The only people who would definitely remember seeing me were Stu and Alysa. So, that leaves Alysa. I don't want to even mention her name. Afraid that any attention to Alysa will lead to more bad things happening.

"I don't know if anyone else saw me. I just talked to Stu and then left." I shrug. My stomach is curdling and I feel sweat soaking through the arm pits of my white shirt. She nods her head and writes in her notepad.

"It would appear he took some drugs with the alcohol. You know what sort of drugs he'd be taking? Did he do drugs when you were together?

I shake my head. "No, I don't remember him ever taking drugs. Booze, sure. But he wasn't a big drinker either. I mean, once in a while, he would drink a lot. But drugs, I don't know. I wasn't aware of him doing any."

"You know anything about prescription drugs? Any of your friends doing that sort of thing at parties?"

"I don't know." I wonder if she can tell that I can't catch my breath. The room feels small. Very small and claustrophobic now. If she ever found out that I gave Alysa pills, what would happen to me?

"Can you see my concern, though?" Officer Maloney asks, leaning forward. "First Fitz, now Stu. Do you pray Miss Tiller?"

I blink. Thrown off by her question. "Uh, sure. Sometimes."

"I suggest you say some prayers for your ex-boyfriend. You better pray that he survives. Or we have a second death in one school within a month. That will warrant a full investigation."

I nod.

She rises from the chair. "You can head back to class," she tells me, opening the office door and returning to her chair where she waits quietly until I'm gone.

It's second period, and I can barely keep my eyes opened with the pain in my head. But I need to speak to Alysa. Find out what she has said, what she knows. Silently, I curse my mom for leaving my phone dead. I can't even text her. I decide to go to the library to rest my head on a desk until the period is over. I can't believe it when I see her scribbling furiously on a table in the middle of the library.

"Alysa," I drop my hand on her shoulder. She jumps and jerks her head toward me.

"What the fuck?" Her eyes are wide and her mouth in a scowl. "You trying to scare the crap out of me?" I roll my eyes.

"Of course not."

"Why haven't you answered any of my texts. I've sent, like, a thousand. Did you hear about Stu? And did you get me more pills yet? I'm on empty now."

I wonder how she can ask those two questions in the same breath. Has she always been this cold-hearted? I'm sure the answer is no. She's changed dramatically in the past year. Her eyes are hollowed out by black rings and she has a smattering of pimples on her chin that I hadn't noticed two days earlier. She stares at me impatiently, waiting for an answer.

"I assume you haven't slept, yet," I say.

"Hell, no," Alysa looks at me and grimaces. "You look like shit."

"I look like shit? Look in the mirror. At least I'm sick. What's your excuse?" I spit back, then shake my head. This is not going in the direction I want. "Listen, tell me what happened at Stu's after I left. How did this happen?"

"Can you believe he's in a coma?" Her eyes widen as she breathes slowly out her mouth. "I don't know what happened. He was fine one minute and a wreck the next. Then I left."

"You left him a wreck? What does that mean? How was he a wreck? Did he take the pills too?"

She shrugs, dropping her pencil on the paper in front of her. "I don't remember. I think he did. I think I offered one or two to him."

I pull out the chair beside her and sit down, grab her hands. "You need to fucking remember, Alysa!" Then lowering my voice to a raspy whisper. "The cops are back and they're asking questions. What do you know?"

"I told you what I know. I don't remember anything else. I'm telling the truth. Shit, I drank a lot after you left. I kinda blacked out after, um..." Her voice trails off.

I shake her arms. "After what? Tell me what happened." Alysa picks up her pencil and begins reading the paper in front of her.

"Nothing happened," she replies. "He'll be fine." She looks up at me, her dark eyes cool. "Where are the pills you said you'd get me." I'm so frustrated and angry, it takes all my self-control to not grab her by the neck and strangle her. Then I remember the monster inside of me. Don't want to keep giving into the hate. Why does she have to make it so hard?

"I never said I'd get you more pills. I texted you that I'm not getting you anymore. That was it. You're on your own."

"You can't do that to me! I won't let you." She grabs my arm as I rise. I pull her arm off of me and squeeze it hard.

"Ouch!" She cries. When I let go, I see blood soaking through her sleeve.

"What the heck?" I say.

"Shit, Lana." She gets up from her chair and runs out of the library. I start to follow her, but decide against it. Talking to her is getting me nowhere. I turn to look at the paper she was working on. It's a university scholarship application. The paper is covered in pencil marks that have been written and erased several times. Now, there's a smudge of blood on it, too. Why would her arm be bleeding? That must be one heck of scratch if it bleeds that easily. I shudder to consider what kind of hot mess her life has become. Probably, I realize, not that different from my own. She's authored two terrible lives. Mine. And her own. I stand to leave but my head is spinning faster than ever. The room is growing dim. Then there's just black.

Chapter 20

One of the Good Lunatics

I wake up in a slightly darkened room, my cheek against a wet pillow. Blink a few times before I figure out I'm in the school office on a cot. The pillow is wet from my own sweat. I wonder how I got here, as I don't remember anything after seeing Alysa. Slowly, I lift myself up so I'm sitting. My head is hurting a little less, but I'm still dizzy.

"You're awake." The secretary steps into the room and stands in front of me. "How are you feeling?"

"I'm okay," I answer, rubbing the back of my head. "How did I get here?" I try not to look at her green dress. It's too bright for my eyes.

"Oh dear, you don't remember walking here?" she asks. "That's not good. The librarian saw you fall and helped you get back up and walked you to the office."

I don't remember any of that. Lifting my eyes to the clock, I see that an hour has passed since I talked to Alysa. Has she been interrogated by Maloney, I wonder.

"Weird," I answer. "I think I'm okay now. Can I leave?"

The secretary lifts her palms. "No, I don't think that's a good idea. You still look pale. We're trying to get a hold of your parents to come pick you up."

"My parents? Please don't call them. They don't need to be bothered with this. I'm fine. Really. And, I can call them on my own."

"Okay, I'll leave that up to you. But I think you should wait at least ten minutes before you go anywhere. You don't want to pass out again. Obviously, you're sick." I suddenly feel exhausted again and nod my head. Maybe a few more minutes lying down would be good for me. She exits the room and I suddenly remember I brought my charger for my phone. Eyeing an electric outlet beside the cot, I reach for my bag by my feet and pull out the phone and charger. Within a few minutes, the screen is alight.

I have fifteen texts from Demit and forty-one from Alysa. Two from my mom. I quickly review Demit's texts and see he hasn't sent anything since we spoke this morning. I text him now.

LANA: Hey, in the office now lying down. I think I fainted in library and blacked out. Was talking to Alysa just before it happened. Before that was interrogated by cop again. Awful morning. I feel like hell and want to die. Seriously. Help!
DEMIT: Oh no! That's awful. U ok? How was the cop? U have nothing to hide. Did nothing wrong. U should go back home and sleep.

LANA: I don't want to go home. My mom will hide my phone from me. She's so annoying trying to figure out what's going on in my life. I worry she will start snooping and read my texts. I wd die!!

DEMIT: K. Go to my house. It's empty. Nobody will be home until at least 4. There's a key in the garage under the stack of flower pots.

LANA: Really? That would be awesome. U sure????

DEMIT: Of course. Go sleep in my bed. I'll be home around 3. Get better. And stop worrying so much!!!

LANA: I'll stop worrying once I find out what happened with Stu and when Alysa stops begging me for pills. Things are very strange with her. I think she's losing her mind

I regret the text the second I hit send. Completely forgot that Demit's father has gone crazy. Groaning, I consider sending an apology. But what would I text? *Oops, I forgot your dad is a lunatic, too. I'm sure he's one of the good lunatics out there.* The damage is done. Just let it ride.

DEMIT: Yeah, she's crazy all right. No doubt. I'll talk to her later today. Try to reason with her about the stupid pills. I wouldn't worry about Stu. It's not your problem. Remember what he did to you. Maybe he deserves what he got. I know that sounds mean, but so be it. Forget about him. U have enough to worry about.

Setting the phone on the cot beside me, I lie back down and close my eyes. It's hard not to think about Stu. And Fitz, for that matter. Two ex-boyfriends. Both responsible for doing horrible things to me. One is dead, the other in a coma. Both seem to have overdosed on something.

I don't want to connect anymore dots. Nobody wanted them dead more than I did, except maybe one person. But Demit would never do something like that. *Would he?*

Demit had access to drugs. He knew that they'd both hurt me in one way or another. I remember the look on his face when I got in the car Saturday night. The accusations. Could he have been so jealous and angry that he visited Stu later that night? Somehow put drugs in his drink? Cut him with a knife? I shake my head. It's too implausible. Unless he used the gun? Forced them to do what he demanded. I bend my knees into my chest. Bile is rising from my nauseous stomach. I force it back down, and let myself fall asleep.

When I wake up, another hour has passed. This time, my head is no longer aching so I rise from the cot and grab my phone. It's fully charged now. Awesome. I quickly review the last few texts from Alysa.

> *ALYSA: I hear you're sick. Passed out or something. That sucks. Have u talked to Demit? Need the pills asap*
> *ALYSA: U still in the school? We need to talk. Need the pills. Dying here.*
> *ALYSA: Forget it. I'm meeting Demit later today. You're off the hook for now.*
> *ALYSA: Meeting the cop later today I think. Hmmmm. Better make sure Demit knows to bring the pills. Don't want me to tell cops about your blog do u?*
> *LANA: Go to hell*

I drop the phone in my bag. So much for not giving into the hate, but she fills me with such fury. Making her ridiculous demands. Acting like she owns me. I'll let Demit talk to her.

At least then he'll get an idea of what kind of psychopath I'm dealing with. I need to stop worrying. That's one thing Demit said that I can fully agree with. At least for a couple hours. I sign out of school and wave goodbye to the secretary. She asks if I have a ride home. I reply yes and walk out the door.

***

I toss and turn in Demit's bed for about an hour, then give up on trying to sleep. The painkillers I'd found in his bathroom have started to kick in now, anyways, and I feel almost normal. Wishing I'd brought my laptop, I look at my website from my phone. There are seventeen comments on my last blog post. I decide to read them later. It's very likely I will get Demit to shut everything down before the end of today, so why bother reading them? Tapping on my messages, I finally read Mom's texts.

> MOM: *What's going on? I got a phone call that ur sick. Do you need me to drive u home? At work now.*
> MOM: *Still waiting to hear back from you. Assuming u r fine now?*
> MOM: *If ur going home, bought lots of fresh fruit. Have an orange! New knife is still in package. I think on front hall desk. Text me pls!!*
> LANA: *I'm fine. Will b home later this aft. Don't worry.*

Walking downstairs into Demit's kitchen, I realize I'm starving. I open the refrigerator and pull out a carton of orange juice and a jar of jam. I feel like having a peanut butter and jam sandwich. After opening a few cupboards I find everything I need to make it. Setting it on a white plate, I notice a serrated knife on the counter that I use to slice the sandwich in half. Holding it in the air, I stare at it for a few seconds after using it. A door seems to open inside my head, letting in a whiff of understanding. Dropping the knife, I pull out my phone and read Mom's text again.

The paring knife is still missing, that's why she replaced it. Trying to remember when they first started blaming each other for its disappearance, I think it was the Saturday morning. Alysa had been in my kitchen the night before. And Demit? I suppose he could have stolen it, too. A few days earlier. If anyone took the knife, it was definitely gone before Saturday night. Brought to Stu's party?

A flash of red comes to me. Alysa's sleeve, soaked in blood when I grabbed her forearm. Did she cut herself with a knife? The same knife that was used to cut Stu? I slam my fist on the counter. I'm thinking like a crazy person. How would she ever cut Stu? He's twice her size. I wish I'd asked Officer Maloney about the cut. Where it was. How big a cut was it? What if he cut himself? But that makes no sense either. Why would he do something like that? The questions are rushing in like waves, crashing into my brain, but leading nowhere other than a raging sea of confusion. *Shut up.* I try to silence them as I eat my sandwich. My phone dings. A new text from Demit.

DEMIT: *Are you awake?*
LANA: *Yep. Eating a sandwich.*
DEMIT: *ok. Got news on Stu.*
LANA: *Yeah? What is it?*
DEMIT: *He's dead.*

I read the words again. Unable to believe them. Dead? A cold draft has suddenly invaded my body. I drop to the floor and wrap my shivering arms around my shins, tucking my head into my knees. This can't be happening. I feel responsible. As though all the horrible things that have been happening to me have somehow been projected onto all those around me. Who will die next, I wonder morbidly. And, how soon before the cops decide to charge me with murder?

> LANA: I can't believe it.
> DEMIT: I know. Crazy. I'll be home soon. Am meeting Alysa after school to talk. K?
> LANA: K

I feel helpless. Like somehow, I've played a role in this horrible outcome and yet, there's nothing I can do to make it all stop. I notice a desktop computer in the living room through the kitchen doorway. Walking to it, I move the mouse and watch the screen light up. I can write one final blog post. Not sure what I'll write, but decide to sit down, place fingers on the keyboard and see if anything comes.

October 28, 2013

The End is Near

Two people are dead and, for the record, I didn't do it. You know that saying too close for comfort? Well, this is one of those times when a meaningless saying suddenly makes complete sense. My life has gotten messy. Scary frigging outta control messy.

I keep running the same questions through my head. How did this happen? And why am I in the middle of it? If this is the bad dream I wish it was, then now would be an ideal time for me to wake up. (Cue the arm pinch... ouch.)

I'm scouring my mind to connect the dots. Struggling to even find the dots. All I wanted was to be myself. To finally stop caring about what other people wanted of me.

And just. Be. Me.

When I started this blog, I promised to tell my story. At that time, I'd wanted revenge. Yah, I admit it. I was angry. Bad things were happening to me, so why not want bad things to happen to all the people who were out to ruin my life? Now all I want is my happy ending. I gave up the need for revenge a long time ago.

Stupid me. Thinking if I'd learned to be myself, everything else would fall into place. But no. The truer lesson is that life doesn't work out the way we want it. No matter how hard I tried to rewrite my story, I couldn't do it. There are too many twists, characters, and plot lines. I've lost control. Maybe I never had any in the first place.

This story is no longer just about me. And it sure as hell isn't written by me. There's a larger hand at play. Everything is driving toward a horrible tragic conclusion. So I'm making this blog post very simple. One request to the hands at play. If you are reading this, please let no one else die.

Chapter 21

Cuts Like a Knife

Demit hasn't come home yet and I haven't received a text from him since he told me about Stu's death. I feel paralyzed. Like I can't go home and I can't go to school. I'm afraid to walk anywhere for fear the police are looking for me. I'm hanging on to a crazy hope that Alysa didn't tell the cops anything about me since she knew she would be meeting Demit after school. Surely, she can, at least, wait to see if he would supply her more drugs. Because that's what all this is about for her, isn't it?

I text Demit for the fifth time in the past hour.

Where r u?

He finally responds this time.

DEMIT: In car with Alysa and Sarah. Going to her place now. Things were getting too heated at school and a teacher was starting to walk over. So we took off.

LANA: What? Don't go with her! She's crazy.
DEMIT: LOL. I'm a big boy. I can handle myself. Just
stay in my room. My mom won't even know ur there.
C u soon.

My nerves are taut with tension and fear. It's ridiculous that I'm fearful for Demit. What could she possibly do to him? My stomach feels like a snow globe, its contents shaken and unsettled. I run to the bathroom and throw up the peanut butter sandwich that I'd eaten only an hour ago. My gut is warning me that Alysa has been behind Fitz and Stu's death. And, quite likely, Demit may be her next victim. After washing my mouth out with tap water, I go upstairs to Demit's bedroom and look for his gun. He'd once pointed out that he hid it in the bottom desk drawer. I open it and lift a small stack of books onto the floor. Reaching my hand to the back, I feel a cold handle. Got it. Stuff it in the back of my pants like they do in the movies, and head to Alysa's house.

I decide to borrow Demit's bike because the walk would take too long. Something tells me I need to get there quickly, even as my more practical voice accuses me of being the biggest lunatic of them all. My phone dings as I sit on the bike seat. I quickly look at it. A text from my mom.

A policewoman is here looking for you. Where r u?

My chest tightens. Alysa must have told them something. Why else would they want to ask me more questions? I need to find out the truth before it's too late. Visions of me in an orange prison suit parade through my mind. *My life is over.*

I hear Alysa and Demit arguing as I ride up the driveway of her house and dismount from the bike. Leaning it against the side of the house, I quietly step toward the front door which is wide open. Now that I've arrived, I'm not sure what to do. I edge along the house until I'm just outside the front entranceway and listen.

"There's no deal here!" Demit is yelling now.

"You'd rather your girlfriend go to jail? Is that what you're saying?" Alysa cries back. "Just get me the fucking prescription and this can all end for everyone."

"Lana doesn't want to be your slave. Not today, not ever. And I won't do it either. We already did it once. Now you want more. And when this refill is done, you'll want more. When does it stop?"

"Did it ever occur to you that Lana actually might be guilty? That I've been protecting her all this time?" Alysa asks, calmly now. My heart is beating wildly. *How dare she accuse me of doing any wrong!* I fight my desire to step into the entranceway and instead stay put, listening to what she has to say.

"This is so stupid I can barely stand to listen to you anymore," Demit is laughing harshly. "Just shut up."

"The knife used to cut Stu is from Lana's own kitchen," Alysa says. "I have it! She may have grabbed her scarf but she left the knife. The idiot."

"What are you talking about?" Demit asks. I was right. It was my knife that was used on Stu.

"She probably told you she stayed for a few minutes then left. Sure she left. But did she mention she came back with a knife later that night? That she was part of the partying? Why do you think she was so sick Sunday? It wasn't the flu, you idiot."

"You're a liar!" Demit yells. I hear him walking toward the door. "Stay out of her..." I don't hear him finish the sentence. It sounds like glass shattering and a thump. I step into the doorway. Demit is lying in a heap on the hardwood floor of their hallway. Alysa is standing a few feet back with clenched hands pressed against her forehead. Broken glass glimmers around Demit.

"What the hell?" I stare at Alysa who finally notices me standing before her. She drops her hands to her sides.

"Oh hey, Lana," She says calmly. "He is a very unreasonable person. How can you stand it?"

I drop my knees to the floor as Demit starts to stir. "You're crazy! You could've killed him."

"I'm crazy?" She laughs. "You're the one who's going to go to jail for killing Fitz and Stu. I spoke to the cops today. Told them about the knife. That you were the one who carved lines on Stu's body."

"What are you talking about? What lines? Why would you tell such horrible lies about me?"

"I told them I would get them the knife. I told them I have it. And I'm sure they'll quickly realize it came from your house."

"The blood on your arm," I say to myself. "That blood is from you cutting yourself. I don't get it. Did you get him to cut himself? Did you both cut yourselves?"

"You're such an idiot. You were always so much stupider than me. Yet somehow you always came out looking better than me. I'll never understand it. Yes, I cut myself. We were drinking gin and I popped a couple pills. Stu was so drunk by then he barely noticed when I gave him two. It was all just fun, you know? Then it was easy to give him the knife and get him to try cutting. All I had to do was dare him. Do you know how stupid guys are when they're drunk? They'll do anything if you dare them." She rolls her eyes. "I shouldn't tell you all this, but what the hell. He went upstairs, thinking I'd left. But I hadn't. As soon as he was snoring, I cut a couple more lines on him. One horizontal line, one vertical line. A capital L."

"What?" I can't believe I'm hearing this. Despite speaking nonchalantly, the right side of her face is twitching madly. "You killed him."

She shakes her head viciously. "No. Wrong." Demit is sitting up now, so I rise to standing. "I didn't kill him. That was an accident. His dad found him as he was suffocating on his own vomit."

"It was your fault!"

"No!"

"And what about Fitz?" I ask. "Was that your work, too?"

"They were both accidents. I'm not a killer," Alysa waves her hand. "You're a killer, Lana. At least that's what the cops will think once I give them the knife. But this can all go away. I won't say another peep about the knife. Just supply me with my pills until I get my university acceptance letters. That's all. Another couple months. I swear!"

"That's what this is all about? Getting into university? You're ruining all these lives so you can get into a university program?"

Alysa sighs deeply, her shoulders droop. "Don't you get it? Have you met my fucking parents? One is a psychiatrist and the other is a brain surgeon. Do you think they're okay with me being average?" She scowls as she annunciates the last word. "I need to have at least ninety-five in every course. The last time I brought home a mark lower than ninety-five, my mom laughed at me. I told her I studied for hours and I'm sorry it wasn't high enough. And she laughed at me, like I'm some kind of joke. Then she threw it in the garbage without saying a word."

"I don't believe you. You're a liar. And you're sick."

Alysa tips her head back and laughs, "It's all true. Ironic, isn't it? That my parents are so busy fixing other people's fucked up brains that they can't even see their own daughter is having a nervous breakdown?"

"But why go after me? Why am I any part of this? I thought we were best friends."

"You were just another reminder of what I couldn't be. I could never look as pretty as you. Or get the guy. I was always the second choice. Always a little fatter. Always a little uglier. You got to live this charmed life. Guys loved you everywhere we went. Fitz could never stop staring at you, even while we were dating. And Stu was another one. He would have done anything to have you back."

"That's not true. None of that is true."

"You're an idiot. Of course it's true. I tried to like you. I really did, over the past few years, but everything changed in high school. And I started to hate you. I'm sorry, but I did. I wanted you to suffer the way I have. But I can put all that behind me now. I swear I can. Just give me my pills."

I look at Demit who is now standing next to me. He's shaking his head. "The pills are making you worse, not better," he says. "You're completely crazy."

"So what," she retorts. "Please, please, please," she begs, clasping her hands before her chest. "Just give me what I need."

"Where's the knife?" I ask, slipping my hand to the back of my jeans.

"You think I'm going to just give it to you?" She shakes her head. "No way. I'll keep the knife until I no longer need the pills. You supply and I keep quiet."

"Not good enough." I pull the gun from my waistband, hold it with both hands and point it at her. My hands are trembling, even though I know it's not loaded. I hear Demit catch his breath beside me.

"Whoa," Alysa lifts her hands into the air. Her eyes skirt from the gun to Demit and back to the gun. "What the fuck, Lana. Take it easy. I'll get the knife."

"Where is it?" I ask. She inches past me and Demit, motioning that it's outside. We follow her to the front step where she bends over, raises a flat stone from the garden, and lifts the knife wrapped in a green kitchen towel.

"Here." She hands it to me. I take it and pass it to Demit. Lowering the gun, I breathe a sigh of relief.

"God, Lana. You say I'm crazy?" Alysa says. "What the hell. I was only joking about telling the cops. I didn't mention the knife at all."

"I don't know what to believe anymore. I just want to put all this behind me," I say, lifting the gun up, I shake it in my hand. "There are no bullets in it, anyway. It's completely harmless. See?" I aim the gun at her and pull the trigger.

"Don't!" Demit yells.

A shot comes out, jerking me back. I step one foot behind the other to catch my balance. Alysa drops to the ground, crumpled over the front walkway. Blood spreading across her white shirt and a pool of red creeping across the stones beneath her. I drop the gun, stunned, as Demit leaps to Alysa's side, pressing the green kitchen towel against her chest.

"Oh my god," I'm too shocked to move. "I didn't mean to," I say, almost pleading. "I thought there were no bullets. You said there were no bullets, Demit."

"Oh fuck, Lana," Demit says in a coarse whisper. Blood soaks through the towel he's holding.

"Is she dead?" Tears spill down my cheeks.

"No, she's still breathing, but barely." Demit hasn't looked up at me yet.

"She's going to live," I say. I have to say it. I have to believe it. "It was an accident. I didn't mean to shoot her."

Demit finally looks up at me. "It was an accident." He reiterates, locking eyes with me. "Call nine-one-one." I nod and pull my phone from my pocket, dial emergency. Tell the operator someone has been shot. We need an ambulance. Here's the address.

"Do you think they'll know it was an accident?" I ask. "What if I go to jail? For Fitz's death, Stu's death? And..."

"She's not dead," Demit says. I look at Alysa. Her eyes are closed and her chest is no longer heaving.

"Save her Demit," I cry. "Don't let her die."

Alysa's head slumps to the side as Demit tries to lift her onto his lap. He presses his ear to her mouth, then looks up at me. There's still a beat.

"You have to go," Demit tells me. "Don't stop at your house. Just go. I'll meet you in the field behind the coffee shop under the hydro lines. You know where I mean?" I nod.

"But what about Alysa?" My voice sounds tinny, as if it's coming through a cheap speaker.

"An ambulance will be here soon. They'll rush her to the hospital and then we will see if she survives."

"Will I go to jail?"

"Maybe." He cocks his head to the side. "We can't take the chance. You need to go."

"Just run away?" It doesn't seem right. But neither does going to jail. I can't think straight, so I do as Demit instructs me. "You'll meet me?" I ask.

A woman in red track pants and a navy jacket walks by with a dog and stops to stare. "Oh my god!" she yells.

I don't take a second look at her. Picking up Demit's bike, I ride as fast as I can away from the scene. *You said there were no bullets.* The phrase plays over and over in my mind. I can't think of anything else as I pedal to the field. There's no space for any other thoughts.

***

"I'm going to jail," I say matter-of-fact.

"No, it was an accident," Demit reminds me when he shows up at the field fifteen minutes after me.

"But this doesn't look like an accident. Nobody will believe me."

"That's why we have to get out of here. We need to go."

"But where?"

"We need to disappear."

I shake my head. What does he mean? Go where? There's only one place for me now. I'm going to jail. I'm going to spend the rest of my adulthood in prison.

"We're going to get in my mom's car and drive. I told her I need to borrow it. She doesn't know that I'm taking off, but once we cross the border, I'll leave the car somewhere and let her know where to get it. I have friends in New York City. Hopefully they can help us out until we come up with a real plan."

I finally understand what he's telling me. "You mean, I'm going to be on the run? Like a fugitive?"

Demit nods. "Yeah. Like that." The fog in my mind clears just enough to understand what he's saying.

"You're coming with me?" I ask.

Demit nods again. "I can't leave you, Lana. I won't let anything bad happen to you. Ever."

Chapter 22

Starting at the End

We walk along the sidewalk until we reach the middle of the bridge. Snow drifts around us as we take in the skyline of downtown Buffalo. I never went back home, never said good bye to my parents. It wasn't worth the risk to get clothes and my passport. Instead, I emptied my bank account and Demit grabbed clothes for both of us before we drove toward the U.S. His sister's passport, incredibly, got me across the border with no problem. My last blog post was published a few hours ago. Demit and I decided to leave the website live for now. There isn't anything on it that I need to worry about. It's simply the truth.

"Where's your cell phone?" Demit asks, pulling his from the pocket of his jacket.

"Got it, here." I lift it up. My mom sent dozens of texts over the past two hours. First demanding me to get home, then pleading with me to come home, then asking for a simple return text.

"We have to get rid of the phones. We need to disappear."

My throat tightens as I nod. Demit wraps his arms around me and pulls me so close against his chest that I begin to believe there's hope somewhere in our future. We separate long enough to send our final texts. I finally respond to my mom, telling her that I'm fine. That it was a horrible accident and I will reach out again in a bit. I don't tell her what a bit really means because I don't know, myself. I'm about to shut the phone off when one final text pops up.

Love you

I turn to him and lift my face to meet his. He kisses me so sweetly that it eliminates my sadness long enough to lift our phones over the railing of the bridge and throw them in.

"It's just you and me now," Demit rests his arm around my shoulder and kisses the top of my head. We stare out into the grey water until the soles of our feet are frozen. And, we have no choice but to move on.

The End.

About the Author

Danielle Leonard is an editor, writer, yoga teacher and mother. Her articles have appeared in various Canadian newspapers and magazines. She is the editor of a lifestyle magazine and lives in the Toronto area with her three teenage sons, dog and cat.